W9-AOM-007

BATMAN TEENAGE MUTANT NINJA TURTLES VOLUME 1

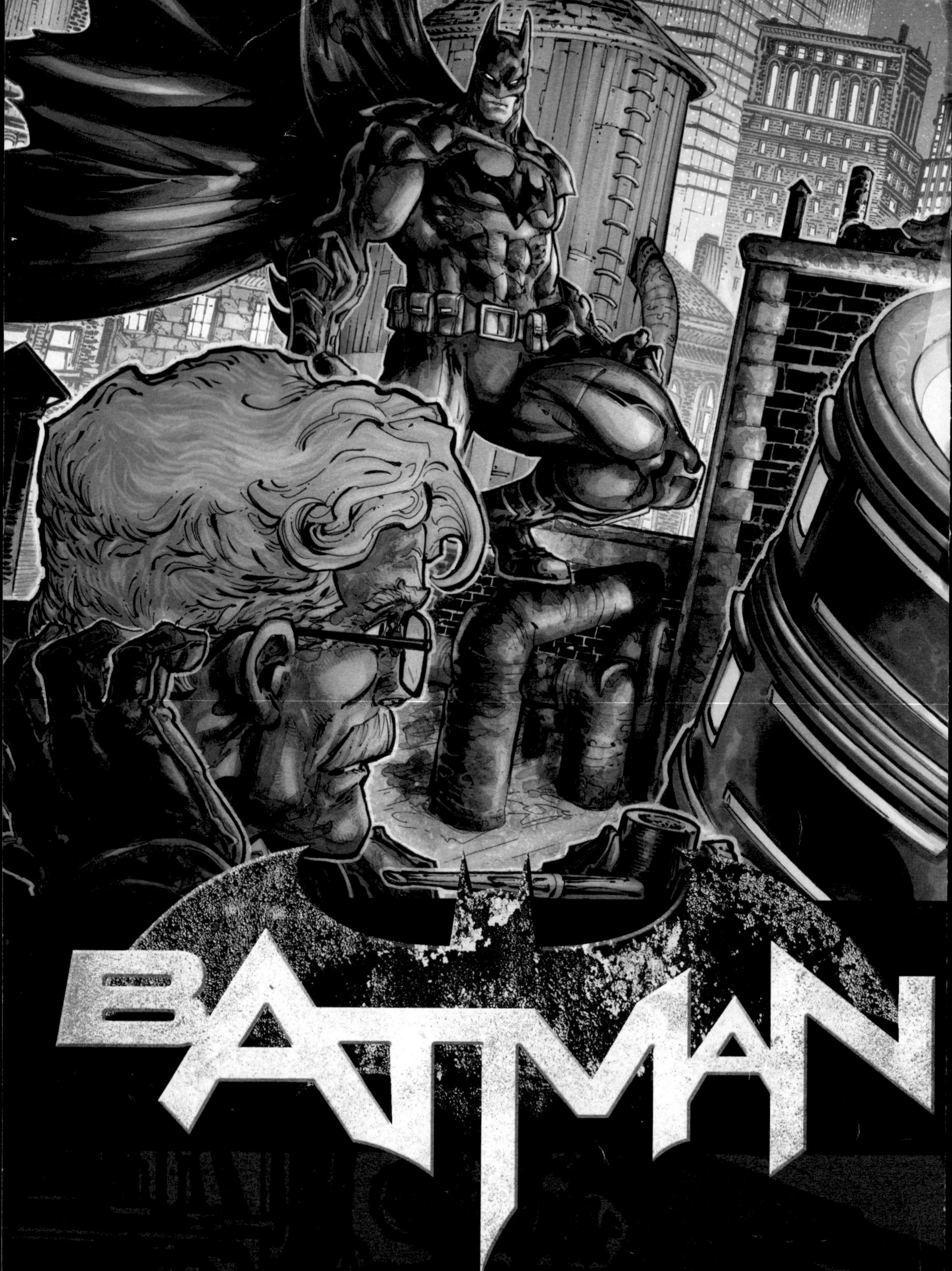
BATMAN

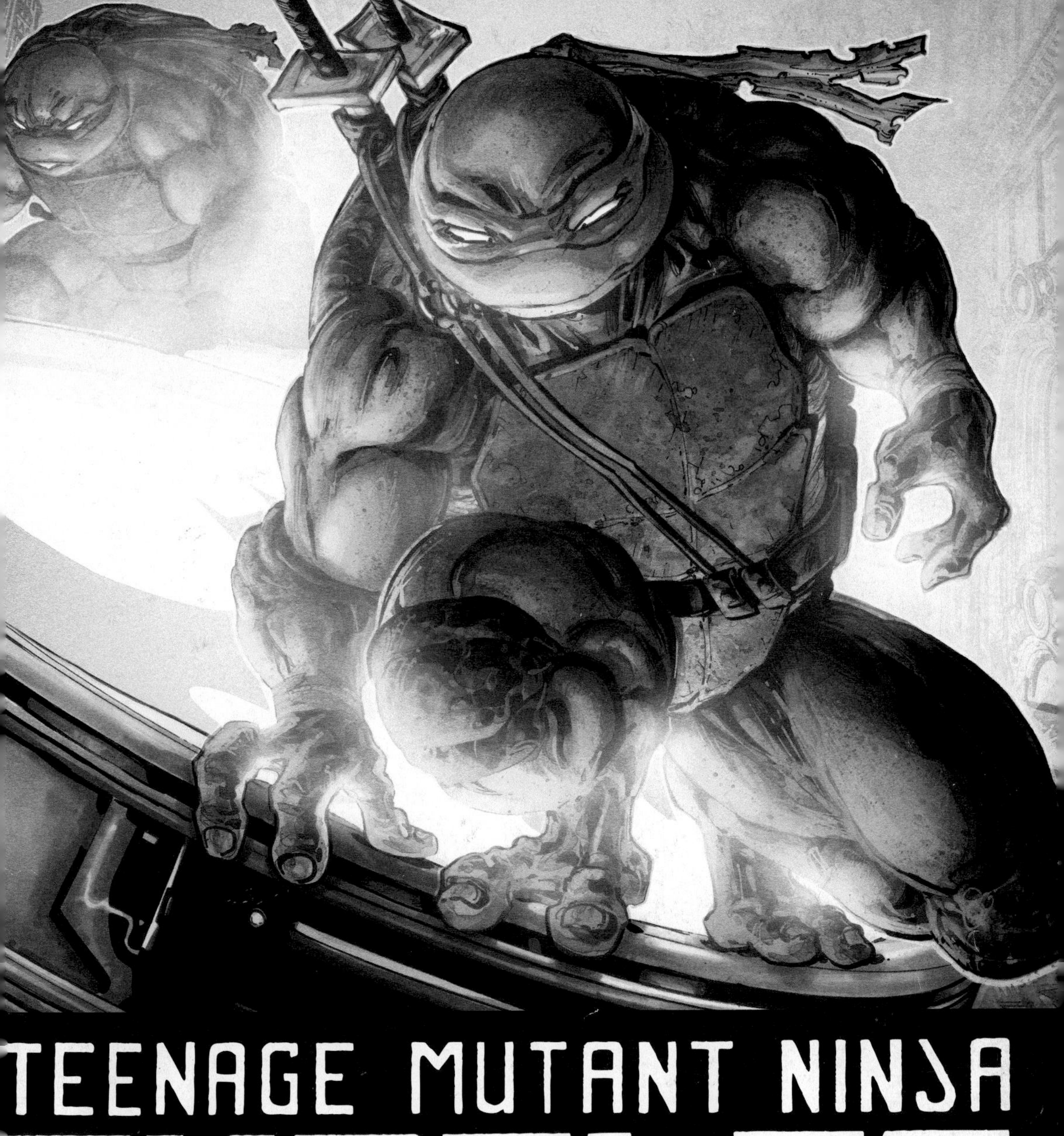

TEENAGE MUTANT NINJA TURTLES

Jim Chadwick Editor – Original Series
David Piña Assistant Editor – Original Series
Jeb Woodard Group Editor – Collected Editions
Paul Santos Editor – Collected Edition
Steve Cook Design Director – Books
Louis Prandi Publication Design

Bob Harras Senior VP – Editor-in-Chief, DC Comics

Diane Nelson President
Dan Didio and Jim Lee Co-Publishers
Geoff Johns Chief Creative Officer
Amit Desai Senior VP – Marketing & Global Franchise Management
Nairi Gardiner Senior VP – Finance
Sam Ades VP – Digital Marketing
Bobbie Chase VP – Talent Development
Mark Chiarello Senior VP – Art, Design & Collected Editions
John Cunningham VP – Content Strategy
Anne DePies VP – Strategy Planning & Reporting
Don Falletti VP – Manufacturing Operations
Lawrence Ganem VP – Editorial Administration & Talent Relations
Alison Gill Senior VP – Manufacturing & Operations
Hank Kanalz Senior VP – Editorial Strategy & Administration
Jay Kogan VP – Legal Affairs
Derek Maddalena Senior VP – Sales & Business Development
Jack Mahan VP – Business Affairs
Dan Miron VP – Sales Planning & Trade Development
Nick Napolitano VP – Manufacturing Administration
Carol Roeder VP – Marketing
Eddie Scannell VP – Mass Account & Digital Sales
Courtney Simmons Senior VP – Publicity & Communications
Jim (Ski) Sokolowski VP – Comic Book Specialty & Newsstand Sales
Sandy Yi Senior VP – Global Franchise Management

BATMAN/TEENAGE MUTANT NINJA TURTLES VOLUME 1

DC Comics, 2900 West Alameda Ave., Burbank, CA 91505
Printed by RR Donnelley, Salem, VA, USA. 7/15/16. First Printing.
ISBN: 978-1-4012-6278-5 (FREDDIE E WILLIAMS II COVER)
ISBN: 978-1-4012-7070-4 (KEVIN EASTMAN AND TOMI VARGA COVER)

Library of Congress Cataloging-in-Publication Data is Available.

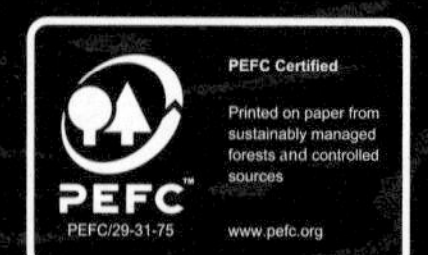

WE COULD HEAR THE GUARDS POUNDING ON THE DOOR, BUT WE COULDN'T MOVE. I COULD SCARCELY BREATHE.
"THE MEN IN BLACK, THEY HAD COME OUT OF THE SHADOWS. WE HADN'T HEARD A THING UNTIL THEY UNSHEATHED THEIR BLADES.
"IT WAS LIKE I HAD FALLEN INTO ANOTHER WORLD. SOME PLACE STRANGE AND IMPOSSIBLE. WE WEREN'T BUILDING WEAPONS, WE DIDN'T DEAL IN DEATH...
"WE WERE THERE TO SAVE LIVES, TO BUILD AN ENERGY SOURCE THAT WOULD BURN BRIGHT AND CLEAN FOR DECADES. A GENERATOR THAT COULD CHANGE THE WORLD.
"BUT THERE WE WERE, AND I KNEW THAT WE WOULD NEVER SEE THAT FUTURE. IT WAS THE END. THE END FOR ALL OF US.

"WHAT HAPPENED NEXT WAS QUICK...I COULD BARELY PROCESS IT...
"OUR IN-HOUSE SECURITY BROKE THROUGH THE DOORS... THE INTRUDERS SEEMED READY FOR THE ATTACK...

"AND THEN THEY CAME.
"A FLASH OF RED...

"BLUE...

"IT SEEMED LIKE THEY WERE FIGHTING THEM. FOR A MOMENT, I THOUGHT I WAS SAVED...BUT AS THE LIGHTS CAME BACK ON, I SAW THE GENERATOR WAS GONE...
"AND I SAW THEM TURN TOWARDS ME, ANGRY...MORE FRIGHTENING THAN ANYTHING I'D FACED THAT NIGHT.

"AND THEN THE LIGHTS CUT OUT ENTIRELY. I THOUGHT IT WAS A POWER SURGE, BUT THERE WAS SOMETHING WRONG IN THE AIR.
"SOMETHING MORE THAN DARKNESS.

"PURPLE...

"ORANGE...
"THERE WAS THE GLINT OF METAL. THE SOUND OF BLADE ON BLADE... FLESH HITTING FLESH.

"I SAW THEIR EYES...THEIR INHUMAN EYES...

I'VE SEEN A LOT OF STRANGE THINGS IN GOTHAM CITY, BATMAN. BUT I'VE NEVER SEEN ANYTHING LIKE THIS...
THE GENERATOR... I CAN'T IMAGINE WHAT IT COULD DO IN THE WRONG HANDS. YOU HAVE TO STOP THEM.
I WILL.

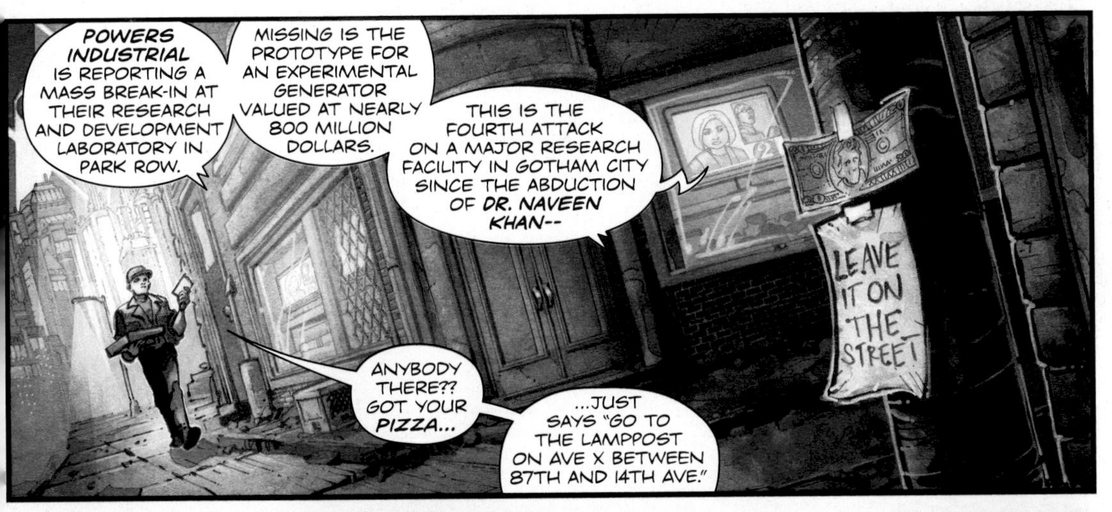
POWERS INDUSTRIAL IS REPORTING A MASS BREAK-IN AT THEIR RESEARCH AND DEVELOPMENT LABORATORY IN PARK ROW.
MISSING IS THE PROTOTYPE FOR AN EXPERIMENTAL GENERATOR VALUED AT NEARLY 800 MILLION DOLLARS.
THIS IS THE FOURTH ATTACK ON A MAJOR RESEARCH FACILITY IN GOTHAM CITY SINCE THE ABDUCTION OF DR. NAVEEN KHAN--
LEAVE IT ON THE STREET
ANYBODY THERE?? GOT YOUR PIZZA...
...JUST SAYS "GO TO THE LAMPPOST ON AVE X BETWEEN 87TH AND 14TH AVE."

--A THEORETICAL PHYSICIST FROM GOTHAM UNIVERSITY-- LATE LAST MONTH.
THE GOTHAM CITY POLICE DEPARTMENT HAS DENIED THAT THE ATTACKS ARE LINKED--
PINA'S PIZZA
ON THE STREET? YOU'VE GOTTA BE KIDDING...
LEAVE IT ON THE STREET
WELL, ALL RIGHT...

BUT THE STREETS ARE QUIET TONIGHT, AS GOTHAM WAITS TO SEE WHAT THESE ATTACKERS MIGHT DO NEXT.
HEY! HEY! QUIT SHOVING!
YOU CAN'T REACH IT.
DUDE, I CAN TOTALLY REACH IT.
PINA'S PIZZA

UH...
PINA'S PIZZA

OKAY. SO I HAVE AN UPDATE. MAYBE I CAN'T REACH IT.
PINA'S PI
SIGH MIKEY...
THERE.

COME ON. WE DON'T WANT TO BE SEEN.
MMMMM...
HEY! THAT'S FOR ALL OF US!
PINA'S PIZZA
"THEY'RE NINJAS."

MASTER BRUCE?
I'M AFRAID I'VE MISPLACED YOU SOMEHOW.

THE LEAGUE OF ASSASSINS, PERHAPS?
THE LEAGUE USES MANY FORMS OF MARTIAL ARTS. FIGHTING STYLES FROM EVERY CORNER OF THE WORLD. THIS CLAN IS MORE SPECIALIZED.
AND THEY DON'T WANT TO BE SEEN.
ISN'T THAT RATHER THE POINT OF BEING A NINJA?
HH.

RA'S WOULD HAVE MADE A PLAY AGAINST ME BY NOW. THIS ISN'T AN ATTACK ON THE CITY ITSELF, THIS IS MORE DELIBERATE.
THIS IS SOMEONE NEW. AND THERE ARE METAHUMANS INVOLVED...SOME KIND OF MONSTROUS CREATURES.
THEY'VE TAKEN FOUR PIECES OF EXPERIMENTAL MILITARY-GRADE TECHNOLOGY SO FAR, BUT NO WEAPONS.
THEY MUST BE BUILDING SOMETHING.
SOMETHING DANGEROUS.

WELL, WE WOULDN'T KNOW ANYTHING ABOUT THAT, NOW, WOULD WE?
WE'RE NOT HAVING THIS ARGUMENT AGAIN, ALFRED.
IT'S HARDLY AN ARGUMENT, SIR. MERELY AN OBSERVATION.
ALFRED...

...
WE'RE NOT DISCUSSING THIS ANY FURTHER, ALFRED. THERE'S WORK THAT NEEDS TO BE DONE.
THERE SHOULD HAVE BEEN A CALL FROM THE GCPD.

OVER HERE.
I'VE GONE OVER THE INJURIES TO ALL THE SURVIVORS OF THE LAST FOUR ATTACKS. THE BRUISING IS CONSISTENT WITH GENERAL FORMS OF NINJUTSU.
IT'S ONE WEEK UNTIL THE ANNIVERSARY OF YOUR PARENTS' MURDER.
EVERY YEAR AT PRECISELY THIS TIME YOU THROW YOURSELF INTO A LITTLE PET PROJECT.
I'M STILL TRYING TO GET THE SCORCH MARKS OFF THE CAVE WALL FROM THE FLAMETHROWER DEBACLE LAST YEAR.
THE INTIMIDATOR SUIT IS MORE THAN A PET PROJECT, ALFRED.
OF COURSE, AND IF YOU HAD ENLISTED LUCIUS FOX'S HELP, PERHAPS YOU WOULD HAVE FINISHED--
I DON'T NEED HELP ON THIS.
OF COURSE NOT.
I SUPPOSE YOU STILL HAVEN'T CONSIDERED CALLING YOUNG MASTER DAMIAN BACK FROM HIS MISSION ABROAD.
HE'S DOING IMPORTANT WORK.
FORGIVE ME, SIR. BUT THIS WEEK IN PARTICULAR I THINK YOU SHOULD BE WITH YOUR FAMILY.
THERE WAS.
THE WAYNE ENTERPRISES R&D FACILITY HAS BEEN ASSIGNED TEN PATROL CARS THIS EVENING FOR ADDED SECURITY.
CALL THEM BACK AND RESPECTFULLY DECLINE.
AND I SUPPOSE I SHOULD JUST TELL THEM, "OUR COMPANY'S NAMESAKE AND PRESIDENT WOULD RATHER THESE STRANGE NINJAS AND THEIR MONSTROUS ASSOCIATES ATTACK, SO THAT HE MIGHT PUNCH THEM IN A BAT COSTUME."
YOU'LL FIGURE SOMETHING OUT.
I'M TAKING THE CAR.

HEY THERE, BATS...
GOOD TO SEE YOU AGAIN.
SO IT WORKS?
'COURSE IT WORKS. PAID EIGHTY THOUSAND DOLLARS FOR THE DAMN THING, DIDN'T I?
DOESN'T MEAN THAT IT WORKS.
LOOK. THIS RED DOT RIGHT HERE? THAT'S THE BATMOBILE, RACING THROUGH GOTHAM CITY...OFF TO SAVE THE DAY...
AND HE'S HEADED RIGHT OUR WAY.
HOW'D YOU KNOW WHERE HE'D GO?
I'M SMART LIKE THAT. FOLKS GET A GLIMPSE OF ME AND THINK OH, THAT KILLER CROC, HE'S JUST BRAWN, NO BRAINS.
BUT THEY'RE WRONG. THOSE LABORATORY RAIDS MEAN THAT'S WHERE BATS WILL BE TONIGHT.
AND GUESS WHICH LAB HAS THE LEAST COP PROTECTION?

WAYNE R&D.
LOTS OF LOOT IN THERE...
YEAH, BUT THERE'LL BE A BAT IN THERE, TOO. WE DO IT MY WAY, AND WE WON'T EVEN HAVE TO FIGHT HIM.
THE PRIZE ISN'T WHAT'S INSIDE THE BUILDING, IT'S WHAT HE'S GOING TO PARK RIGHT OUTSIDE.
I TALKED TO A FEW GUYS ON THE BLACK MARKET, AND THEY SAY JUST ONE SMALL PIECE OF THE BAT'S CAR WOULD GO FOR HUNDREDS OF THOUSANDS.
WE STRIP IT FOR PARTS AND WE'RE GOING TO BE RICH FOR LIFE.
DID WE REALLY HAVE TO COME THROUGH DOWN HERE?
YOU WANT HIM SPOTTING US? NO. THE SEWERS ARE THE WAY TO GO.
THIS BETTER WORK, CROC...WE LEFT A GOOD GIG WITH THE PENGUIN FOR THIS.
IT'S GONNA WORK.
AND HE'S PARKED. PERFECT.
WE CAN GET UP RIGHT THROUGH... HERE?

HUH.
THE HELL IS THIS PLACE?
LOOKS LIKE SOME TEENAGER'S BEDROOM...
WEIRD SPOT FOR THEM TO HANG.
PIZZA'S STILL WARM...

HEY, KIDS, DON'T BE SCARED. I WON'T EATCHA. PROBABLY.
THEY SHOW THEMSELVES, YOU GO FULL LETHAL. WE DON'T WANT THEM RUNNING TO THE COPS. DON'T KNOW WHAT THEY HEARD.
I DON'T SEE ANYTHING.

SAY, THIS LOOKS LIKE A FUN GAME. DEATH LASER PONY RACERS, HUH?

WHOOPS.

NOOO... MY PONY RACERS...
HUSH...

"...EVERYONE GET READY."

YOU KNOW, I'M CURIOUS--
--WHAT WOULD A CLAN OF NINJAS WANT WITH AN EXPERIMENTAL SIGNAL AMPLIFIER?
I'VE GONE THROUGH THE FILES.
EVERYTHING ELSE THAT WAS IN THIS LABORATORY, YOU COULD HAVE TAKEN FROM ONE OF THE LABS YOU'VE ALREADY HIT.
I WANT ANSWERS.
SO. WHO'S READY TO TALK?

MMMPH

WHAT WAS THAT?

WHAT... WHAT ARE YOU?

WE'RE **ALIENS,** BRAH...
SPOOOKY
ALIENS.

WE'RE NOT **ALIENS,** MIKEY.
WELL, I GUESS, IT DEPENDS ON HOW YOU'D DEFINE ALIEN?
FOCUS, GUYS...
I MEAN, WE'RE DEFINITELY NOT FROM **THIS** WORLD--
--BUT WE'RE NOT FROM **OUTER SPACE,** EITHER.
AND HECK, THIS PLACE COULD HAVE A TOTALLY DIFFERENT ETYMOLOGICAL UNDERSTANDING OF THE WORD **"ALIEN,"** FOR ALL WE KNOW.
DONNIE.
I'M JUST SAYING, THESE PLACES ARE DIFFERENT. I MEAN, BACK HOME, THIS WHOLE CITY IS JUST A BIG FIELD RIGHT IN THE CENTER OF THE STATE OF--
RRRRRAAAAGHH...
OH, RIGHT. BIG MONSTER THING.

THIS IS FOR MY PONY RACERS!!!

TELL ME WHAT YOU ARE...

...TELL ME WHAT YOU WANT...
WE... ARE **THE FOOT CLAN.** WE ARE TRYING TO GET HOME...

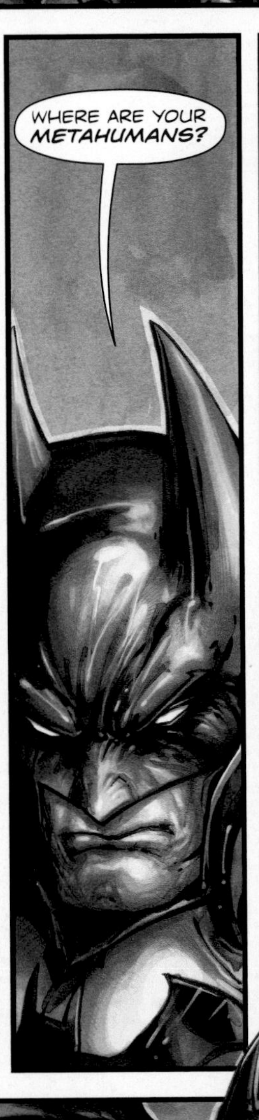
WHERE ARE YOUR ***METAHUMANS?***

META...
...THE ***TURTLES?*** THEY'RE NOT--

UGCK

THIS IS NOT YOUR BATTLE, WARRIOR. OUR SECRETS WILL REMAIN HIDDEN.
LEAVE US BE AND YOUR CITY WILL BE SAFE. CROSS US...

...AND YOU WILL BURN WITH THE REST OF YOUR PEOPLE.
TURTLES...

WELL THAT'S JUST GREAT, ISN'T IT? NOW WE NEED TO FIND A NEW HIDEOUT.
AND YOU THINK THE FOOT JUST WAITED FOR US THEY SLIPPED RIGHT THROUGH OUR FINGERS THE POWERS LAB, AN NOW WHO KNOWS WHE WE'LL GET BACK ON THEIR TRAIL.
WE WERE GOING TO STOP THEM TONIGHT.
SETTLE DOWN, RAPH.
WHY? WE STILL HAVE NO IDEA HOW TO GET HOME. WHO KNOWS WHAT COULD HAVE HAPPENED TO APRIL OR CASEY BY NOW?
MY PRECIOUS BABIES...
SEE, EVEN MIKEY'S UPSET.
WE CAN FIND YOU A NEW GAME, MIKEY.
IT WON'T BE THE SAME!
THEY WON'T LOVE ME LIKE THESE PONY RACERS DID.
YOU'VE DONE WELL, CHILDREN.
MASTER SPLINTER.

BUT RAPHAEL IS RIGHT...
...THIS PLACE IS NOT SAFE FOR US ANYMORE.

SETTLE DOWN, RAPH. IT'S BEEN A LONG NIGHT FOR ALL OF US ALREADY.

LOOK, LEO. I DON'T NEED ANOTHER LECTURE...
THEN STOP ACTING LIKE A BABY! WE'RE ALL IN THE SAME BOAT HERE.
OH MY GOD...

SHE'S BEAUTIFUL...
UH, DONNIE?

I THINK SHE'S TAKEN.
TURTLES...

TEE TEE'S
EVERYBODY RUN! THERE'S A CRAZY GUY IN A BAT SUIT TRYING TO KILL US!
AAHHHH!!!
TEE TEE'S PIZZA
I KNOW, RIGHT? REALLY SPOOKY STUFF.
AW, HEY, DO THESE HAVE ANCHOVIES?
CRUD.
TEE'S

EE's PIZZA
NICE OF YOU TO JOIN US, MIKEY!
I WAS PROTECTING THE CITIZENS, MAN! THE CITIZENS!
THIS GUY IS FIGHTING ON A WHOLE OTHER LEVEL. WE NEED TO STRIKE TOGETHER. OVERWHELM HIM!

YOU'RE WELCOME TO TRY.

OH, CRAP! SORRY! SORRY!

WHAT, YOU THROW ON SOME DUMB HALLOWEEN COSTUME--
--AND THINK YOU CAN **SHOCK** US?
NO. THAT'S WHAT THE ***CAR'S*** FOR.
TASE. LEVEL EVEN.
HEY, ***THINK FAST.***

WHOA. YOU THOUGHT FAST.

WHO'S NEXT?

LOOK, I DON'T KNOW WHO YOU THINK YOU ARE.
BUT YOU NEED TO *BACK* **THE HELL AWAY** FROM MY *BROTHERS.*

THE BREAK-IN AT POWERS...
YOU WERE THERE. YOU WERE A PART OF IT.
WE WERE TRYING TO STOP IT!
ENOUGH.
MASTER SPLINTER...
LEAVE, CHILDREN.

A RAT...
WHAT IS TRULY STRANGER, AN ANIMAL THAT ACTS LIKE A MAN--
--OR A MAN WHO ACTS LIKE AN ANIMAL?
I ADMIRE YOUR DEDICATION TO THE MARTIAL ARTS.
IT IS RARE TO SEE ONE AS WELL-TRAINED AS YOU.

PERHAPS WE'LL BE SEEING MORE OF YOU.

HM.
"THEY CALL HIM BATMAN."

YOU'VE BEEN SURFING THE NET FOR **TWO WEEKS** AND JUST **NOW** YOU FIND OUT ABOUT THE DUDE IN THE BAT COSTUME RUNNING AROUND THIS CITY?
HEY! JUST BE GLAD I FOUND AN INTERNET CAFÉ WITH A **BACK DOOR** THAT'S EASY TO JIMMY OPEN.
THERE'S A **LOT** OF INTERESTING DIFFERENCES BETWEEN THIS WORLD AND OURS! I GOT DISTRACTED.
THERE ARE DIFFERENT MOVIE STARS, DIFFERENT COUNTRIES, HECK, DIFFERENT ELEMENTS...
GUYS. GUYS. WE ARE AGREED ON THE MOST IMPORTANT POINT, RIGHT?

THAT DUDE WAS FREAKING **AWESOME!**
UNLESS HE IS A BAD DUDE. THEN HE IS AT LEAST 40% **LESS** AWESOME.
OR DOES THAT SECRETLY MAKE HIM **MORE** AWESOME?
HMM...I AM GOING TO HAVE TO MAKE SOME CHARTS.
WELL, THE POLICE DON'T SEEM TO BE TOO CRAZY ABOUT HIM, BUT YEAH. HE TAKES DOWN BAD PEOPLE.
THERE'S THIS CLOWN GUY IN PARTICULAR...
SO HE'S A NUT IN A DRACULA COSTUME WHO PUNCHES **CLOWNS.** WHAT'S THE BIG DEAL?

DRACULA COSTUME? WHAT DRACULA MOVIES ARE YOU WATCHING?
DON'T PICK APART EVERYTHING I SAY!
WELL MAYBE IF YOU STARTED MAKING MORE COHERENT REFERENCES.

LOOK. HE WAS JUST SOME LUNATIC, AND NOW HE'S GETTING IN THE WAY OF WHAT WE **SHOULD** BE DOING. WHICH IS GETTING HOME.

WHAT HAPPENS IF SHREDDER AND THE FOOT CLAN MANAGE TO OPEN THAT PORTAL AND WE'RE NOT THERE? WE'RE JUST GOING TO BE STUCK IN THIS CITY FOREVER.
AWAY FROM APRIL. AWAY FROM CASEY. AWAY FROM WHATEVER THE HELL KRANG IS GETTING UP TO NOW THAT HE GOT BOTH US AND SHREDDER OUT OF THE WAY!

THIS GUY WITH THE POINTY EARS--HE'S JUST A DISTRACTION FROM US DOING WHAT WE NEED TO DO.
SO STOP GETTING COMFORTABLE WITH THIS PLACE!
STOP WORSHIPPING SOME WEIRDO IN A COSTUME WHO JUST KICKED ALL OF OUR BUTTS!

AWW, IS SOMEONE GRUMPY BECAUSE THE BATMAN STOLE HIS SAI?
DOES SOMEONE NEED A HUG? OR A PIZZA? OR A PIZZA HUG?
WHAT THE HELL IS A PIZZA HUG?
TRUST ME, YOU DO NOT WANT TO FIND THAT OUT.

LEO. WHAT DO YOU THINK?
...
I'VE NEVER FOUGHT SOMEONE LIKE HIM...SHREDDER, MAYBE... BUT IT WAS DIFFERENT. HE WAS TESTING US. AVOIDING LETHAL BLOWS...HE WANTED TO FIGURE US OUT.

HE WAS FIGHTING LIKE A **DETECTIVE.**
I'VE NEVER SEEN ANYTHING LIKE IT.

AWESOME:
RAD SUIT
LITTLE BAT THROWY THINGS
CAPES
ELECTRO-CAR
KICKED OUR BUTTS
MEAN VOICE
STOLE RAPH'S SAI
OKAY. THAT DEFINITELY GOES ON THE **AWESOME** SIDE OF THE CHART.

NOT YOU, TOO, LEO...I AT LEAST EXPECTED YOU AND MASTER SPLINTER TO BACK ME ON THIS...

FATHER SHOULD HAVE CAUGHT UP WITH US BY NOW. WHERE DO YOU THINK HE IS?

"ANOTHER **DIMENSION,** WAYNE. ANOTH WORLD."

YOU'RE CERTAIN?
I'M AFRAID THERE'S NOT MUCH IN TERMS OF CERTAINTY WITH A READING LIKE THIS. WE'RE IN VERY THEORETICAL TERRITORY. IT'S ALL VERY UNLIKELY.

AS UNLIKELY AS A BILLIONAIRE WITH A RADIOACTIVE WEAPON FROM A KUNG FU MOVIE.
YOU KNOW HOW MUCH OF A CINEPHILE I AM, LUCIUS.
OF COURSE, MR. WAYNE.

WHAT ABOUT IT MAKES YOU THINK THAT WE'RE DEALING WITH OTHER WORLDS?
THE RADIOACTIVE QUALITIES ARE STRANGE, AND FAINT, BUT THEY MATCH THE HYPOTHETICAL QUALITIES OF A TRANS-DIMENSIONAL OBJECT, AS DEFINED BY DR. NAVEEN KHAN.
THE SCIENTIST WHO VANISHED JUST A FEW WEEKS AGO FROM THE UNIVERSITY.

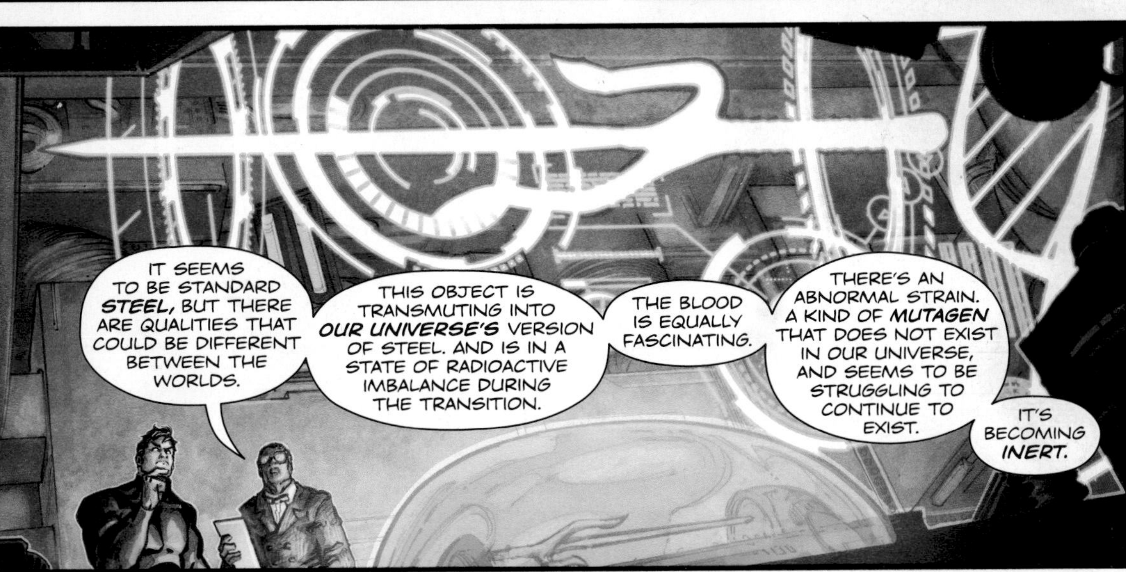
IT SEEMS TO BE STANDARD STEEL, BUT THERE ARE QUALITIES THAT COULD BE DIFFERENT BETWEEN THE WORLDS.
THIS OBJECT IS TRANSMUTING INTO OUR UNIVERSE'S VERSION OF STEEL. AND IS IN A STATE OF RADIOACTIVE IMBALANCE DURING THE TRANSITION.
THE BLOOD IS EQUALLY FASCINATING.
THERE'S AN ABNORMAL STRAIN. A KIND OF MUTAGEN THAT DOES NOT EXIST IN OUR UNIVERSE, AND SEEMS TO BE STRUGGLING TO CONTINUE TO EXIST.
IT'S BECOMING INERT.

SO ANY PHYSICAL CHANGES THAT MIGHT HAVE COME FROM THE MUTAGEN AGENT...
WITHOUT MORE OF IT, I IMAGINE A MUTANT WOULD REVERT TO WHATEVER THEIR NATURAL STATE IS.
THIS IS ALL JUST THEORETICAL, OF COURSE.

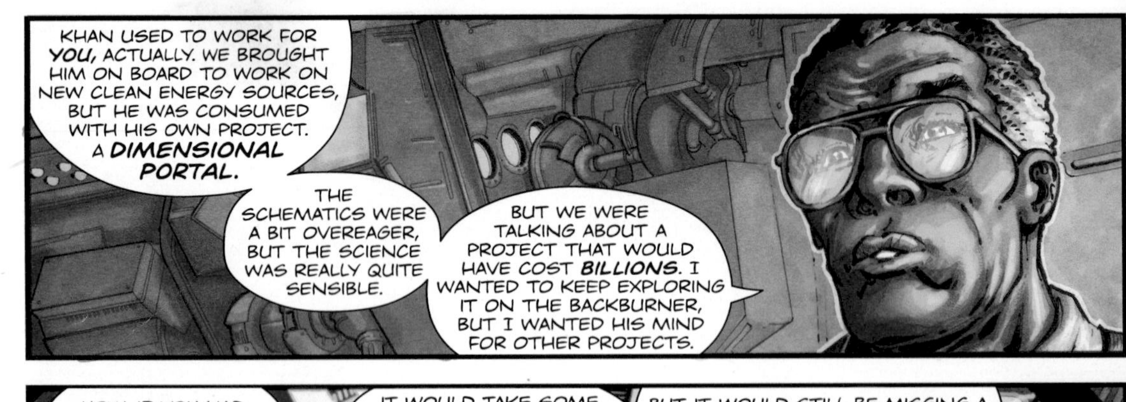
KHAN USED TO WORK FOR YOU, ACTUALLY. WE BROUGHT HIM ON BOARD TO WORK ON NEW CLEAN ENERGY SOURCES, BUT HE WAS CONSUMED WITH HIS OWN PROJECT. A DIMENSIONAL PORTAL.
THE SCHEMATICS WERE A BIT OVEREAGER, BUT THE SCIENCE WAS REALLY QUITE SENSIBLE.
BUT WE WERE TALKING ABOUT A PROJECT THAT WOULD HAVE COST BILLIONS. I WANTED TO KEEP EXPLORING IT ON THE BACKBURNER, BUT I WANTED HIS MIND FOR OTHER PROJECTS.

NOW, IF YOU HAD THESE COMPONENTS, AND A MAN WITH THE INTELLIGENCE OF DR. KHAN...
IT WOULD TAKE SOME DOING, BUT YES, THEY COULD BUILD A POTENTIALLY WORKING MODEL OF WHAT KHAN PROPOSED.
BUT IT WOULD STILL BE MISSING A KEY COMPONENT. A RESONANCE ENGINE, LIKE THE ONE YOU HAD US REMOVE FROM OUR R&D FACILITY BEFORE THE ATTACK THIS EVENING.

WHERE IS IT NOW?
IT'S IN CENTRAL CITY, UNDER A FALSE LABEL, AS YOU SUGGESTED. YOU AND I ARE THE ONLY ONES WHO KNOW IT'S THERE.
I HAD DIFFERENT TEAMS BOX IT AND TAG IT. THERE'S NO WAY TO DETERMINE ITS CURRENT LOCATION WITHOUT THE SERIAL NUMBER I HAVE RIGHT HERE.
THANK YOU, LUCIUS.
I HOPE I DIDN'T STEAL YOU FROM TOO THRILLING AN EVENING.
NOTHING MORE THRILLING THAN A GOOD MYSTERY NOVEL AND A GLASS OF WINE.
BUT IT SEEMS LIKE YOU'LL BE SKIPPING THE GLASS OF WINE TONIGHT.
GOODNIGHT, LUCIUS.

PENNY-ONE. DID YOU GET ALL THAT?
YES, SIR. I'M RUNNING A SEARCH RIGHT NOW.
WE'VE LICENSED THE RESONANCE ENGINE TO FIVE DIFFERENT GOVERNMENT AGENCIES, ALL FOR USE OVERSEAS.
THE DEFENSE DEPARTMENT REPORTED ONE MISSING SIX MONTHS AGO, BUT THEN THE REPORT WAS STRICKEN. THERE'S NO TRACKING ON ITS LOCATION FROM THAT DATE ON.
SO IT'S ON THE BLACK MARKET. AND ALMOST CERTAINLY EN ROUTE TO GOTHAM.
AND THESE STRANGE TURTLE-MEN?
THEY MIGHT NOT BE TURTLE-MEN MUCH LONGER...
WE NEED TO REDOUBLE OUR EFFORTS TO FIND THEM. ACTIVATE SIXTEEN WITCHES EYES AND HAVE THEM RUNNING FULL SCANS ON THE SEWER SYSTEM OF GOTHAM.
I SUSPECT WE'LL FIND THEM IN MIDTOWN, SO START THERE AND BRANCH OUT.
MEANWHILE, I'LL SEE IF I CAN ROUND UP ANY LEADS ON A NEW BUYER OF HEAVY MACHINERY ON THE BLACK MARKET.
IT DOESN'T BODE WELL, THE KIND OF PEOPLE WHO MIGHT BE SELLING A PIECE LIKE THAT.
...
MISTER WAYNE, YOU MAY SEE US SOONER THAN YOU'D THINK.
MUTAGEN INERT

YOU'RE COLORFUL, MR. SHREDDER, I'LL GIVE YOU THAT.
MOST GOTHAM TYPES TAKE A JOB OR TWO BEFORE THEY GET THEIR AESTHETIC TOGETHER. I SEE YOU'RE A MAN WHO KNOWS WHAT IMPRESSION HE WANTS TO MAKE.
I CERTAINLY AM, PENGUIN.

I WAS HAPPY TO MAKE THIS CONNECTION. IT TOOK QUITE A BIT OF MONEY AND A FEW SORDID TYPES. I'M SURE YOU UNDERSTAND.
BUT I THINK YOU'LL BE PLEASED WITH THE PRODUCT.

A WAYNETECH RESONANCE ENGINE.
THE BIRD SAID YOU'D HAVE THE MONEY IN CASH... I DON'T SEE ANY MONEY.

THERE IS NO MONEY.

WHAT?!
THIS IS SOME KIND OF TRICK?! KILL HIM! KILL THEM ALL!
YOUR MEN HAVE ALREADY BEEN DISPOSED OF.

WHAT ABOUT OUR MEN? YOU DON'T KNOW WHO YOU'RE DEALING WITH, HERE...

I DON'T CARE.

IT'S A PITY I WILL HAVE TO LEAVE SO SOON.
THIS CITY SEEMS SO RIPE FOR EMPIRE. SO CAUGHT UP IN ITS PETTY LITTLE POLITICS. THE CRIMINAL UNDERWORLD RUN BY A SAD LITTLE MAN WITH A BIRD'S NAME.
YOU DON'T WANT TO KILL ME!

I KNOW THIS CITY BACKWARDS AND FORWARDS. DO YOU EVEN HAVE ENOUGH POWER TO RUN THESE MACHINES WITHOUT ATTRACTING THE WRONG KIND OF EYES?
DO YOU NEED MORE WEAPONS? MORE MONEY? I CAN TAKE CARE OF ALL OF THAT.
VERY WELL. YOU MAY PROVE AMUSING A LITTLE WHILE LONGER.
SIR... THERE'S NO SIGN OF THE TURTLES, OR THE RAT...
A PITY.
BUT NO MATTER. IF DR. KHAN IS CORRECT, SIMPL LEAVING THEM BEHIND WILL KILL THEM FOR US.

"THERE IS NO WAY FOR THEM TO GET THE UPPER HAND NOW."
MASTER SPLINTER, I DON'T UNDERSTAND...WE'RE GOING TO **DIE?**
FIGURES. THIS CITY WAS BAD ENOUGH **WITHOUT** IT TRYING TO KILL US.

WE WOULD NOT DIE. WE WOULD SIMPLY REVERT TO WHAT WE WERE **BEFORE** THE MUTAGEN.

GAME OVER, MAN...GAME OVER...

FATHER...WHAT ARE WE GOING TO DO? WHY ARE WE WASTING TIME CLIMBING UP THROUGH THE CRACKS OF THE CITY LIMITS?
SHOULDN'T WE BE **OUT THERE?**
WE ARE GOING TO REQUIRE HELP IF WE ARE TO RETURN TO OUR WORLD.
WE CANNOT DO THIS ALONE.

BUT WHO IS THERE TO HELP US?
I BELIEVE THAT WILL BECOME EVIDENT VERY SHORTLY NOW.

OKAY, GUYS... IF I'M DREAMING, NOBODY IS ALLOWED TO PINCH ME UNTIL I GET TO PLAY WITH THAT DINOSAUR.

...e Iceberg Lounge.
IT'S TIME FOR YOU TO GO HOME.
DON'T PRESUME TO COMMAND ME, BIRD MAN.
PENGUIN. THE NAME IS...
NEVER MIND. ALL I MEAN TO SAY IS, WE'VE TAPPED INTO ENOUGH POWER TO ACTIVATE THIS MACHINE OF YOURS. IT MIGHT BLACK OUT THE WHOLE OF GOTHAM CITY, BUT IT WILL WORK.
MY ENGINEERS HAVE BEEN WORKING WITH YOUR SCIENTIST ALL NIGHT. IT'S READY TO GO.
FETCH DOCTOR KHAN IMMEDIATELY. TELL HIM WE'RE READY.
YES, SIR.
IT'S QUITE A VIEW, ISN'T IT?
IT IS.

I LOOK FORWARD TO SEEING MORE OF IT.
WHAT... YOU SAID YOU WERE LEAVING GOTHAM...

WE WILL KEEP THE PORTAL OPEN. I SEE N REASON I CAN' RULE **TWO** CITIES.
I WILL GATHER THE RESOURCES A THE REST OF MEN BACK HO AND RETUR **HERE.**
YOU CAN'T JUST--

IF YOU HAVE A PROBLEM WITH MY PLANS, **BIRD MAN,** I AM HAPPY TO **END** OUR PARTNERSHIP EARLIER THAN SCHEDULED.
NO... NO, OF COURSE NOT.
THAT'S WHAT I THOUGHT.

YOU BELONG TO THE **FOOT CLAN** NOW. DO NOT FORGET IT.
I WILL BE LEAVING A BATTALION OF MY TOP MEN WITH YOU TO **RESHAPE** THIS LURID CASINO INTO THE **FORTRESS** I REQUIRE IN PREPARATION FOR MY RETURN.

DOCTOR KHAN...
PLEASE...I HAVEN'T SLEPT IN FOUR DAYS.
MASTER SHREDDER IS READY FOR YOU TO ACTIVATE YOUR MACHINE.

BUT HE KEEPS CHANGING THE DAMN PLANS...IF HE KEEPS THIS PORTAL OPEN, IT WILL DESTABILIZE REALITY...
...ALL OF GOTHAM CITY MIGHT COLLAPSE INTO IT. HUNDREDS OF THOUSANDS OF PEOPLE COULD DIE!
THAT IS WHAT YOU ARE HERE TO PREVENT, ISN'T IT?
COME NOW.

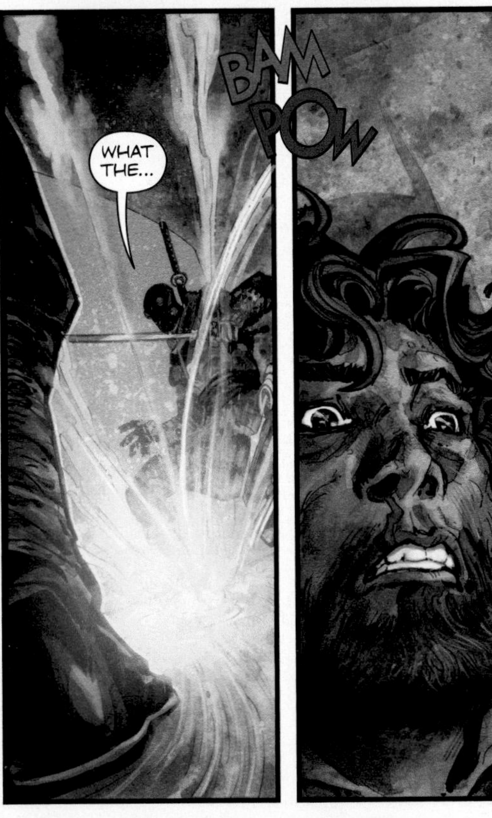
WHAT THE...
BAM
POW

DOCTOR NAVEEN KHAN. THERE'S A BOAT WAITING FOR YOU JUST DOWN THE CORRIDOR. YOU CAN TRUST THE MAN INSIDE. HE'LL TAKE YOU BACK TO THE CITY.
BATMAN... YOU CAN'T DO THIS ALONE.

WHO SAID I WAS ALONE?

THIS IS THE BEGINNING OF A NEW ERA, BIRD MAN. YOU SHOULD BE GLAD TO WITNESS IT...
ALL PREPARATIONS ARE COMPLETE... IT IS TIME TO ACTIVATE THE PORTAL.
MASTER, WE ARE STILL WAITING ON DOCTOR KHAN.
...THERE'S SOMETHING WRONG.

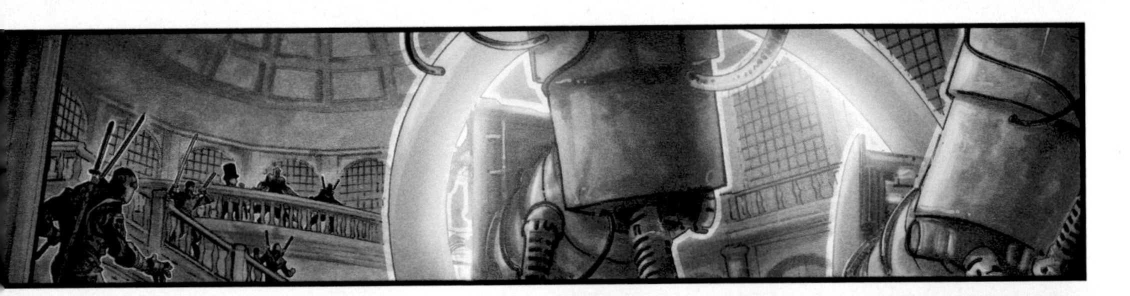

IT'S THE DAMN BAT...

NO, THERE ARE TOO MANY OF THEM...THIS IS THE RAT AND HIS TURTLES...

SORRY TO DISAPPOINT, SHRED HEAD.

BUT THIS HERE IS A...
...TOTALLY AWESOME TEAM-UP!

HOW...

Wayne Manor.
Two Hours Earlier...
SIR, THIS IS NOT QUITE WHAT I HAD IN MIND WHEN I SUGGESTED YOU HAVE SOME DINNER.
I HAD A FEW BITES.
I HEAR THAT'S WHAT FOUR OUT OF FIVE DOCTORS SUGGEST FOR A MUSCLE-BOUND VIGILANTE WHO SLEEPS THREE HOURS A DAY--A FEW BITES AND A DATE WITH THE WAYNE ENTERPRISES LIVE CITY MAPPING PROGAM.
ALFRED.
WE NEED TO FIND THESE MUTANTS. WE'VE BEEN TRACING THE SEWERS FOR HOURS, AND THERE'S NO SIGN. MEANWHILE, THE FOOT CLAN IS ESCALATING THEIR ATTACKS. SIXTEEN BODIES WERE FOUND AT THE DOCKS.
FIVE OF THEM WERE MERCENARIES WITH FALSIFIED BACKGROUNDS. THE CLAN IS MAKING ENEMIES INSIDE AND OUTSIDE OF GOTHAM.
BUT THE MOST ALARMING THING IS THAT IT SEEMS THEY'VE GOTTEN THEIR HANDS ON THE FINAL PIECE OF THE PUZZLE.

THAT'S THE SECONDARY GRID. THE ONE WAYNE ENTERPRISES BUILT IN THE WAKE OF THE ZERO YEAR TO PREVENT THAT KIND OF CENTRALIZED ATTACK IN THE FUTURE.
IT WENT ONLINE 45 MINUTES AGO. THE POWER IS ALL FUNNELING TO THE ICEBERG LOUNGE. I WANTED TO KNOW WHAT I WAS FACING BEFORE I WENT HEAD-TO-HEAD WITH THE FOOT CLAN AGAIN...

BUT THERE'S NO CHOICE. I NEED TO ACT NOW. WE NEED TO GET DOWN TO THE CAVE.
THERE MAY BE A PROBLEM WITH THAT...
WHAT?
THERE'S SOMEBODY DOWN THERE ALREADY.

THIS IS EVERYTHING I HAVE EVER WANTED IN MY ENTIRE LIFE.
MICHELANGELO. WE MUST NOT DISRESPECT THE BELONGINGS OF A MAN WHOSE HELP WE ARE SEEKING.
AW, CAN'T I DISRESPECT THEM JUST A LITTLE BIT LONGER?
NO.
WELL, SOMEBODY SHOULD PROBABLY GET THE MEMO TO DONNIE OVER THERE.
IS THIS WHAT LOVE FEELS LIKE? I'M PRETTY SURE THIS IS WHAT LOVE FEELS LIKE.

I DON'T **LIKE** THIS PLACE, MAN.
THINK OF HOW MUCH MORE EFFICIENT WE WOULD BE IF WE HAD THESE KINDS OF RESOURCES.
NO, YOU ARE MISSING A **CRUCIAL** POINT HERE, LEO--

--THIS PLACE IS **CRAZY!**
THIS IS THE KIND OF THING A **CRAZY PERSON** WOULD BUILD! YOU KNOW...THE KIND OF CRAZY PERSON WHO GOES AROUND AT NIGHT WITH A **MASK** AND A **CAPE** AND A **CAR** THAT **LOOKS** LIKE HIM.

YOU'RE WEARING A MASK.
IT'S **DIFFERENT!** WE'RE LIVING UP TO A **TRADITION.**

THIS GUY, DO YOU THINK HE UNDERSTANDS WHAT'S AT **STAKE** FOR US? WE HAVE **PEOPLE** BACK HOME WHO MIGHT **DIE** IF WE DON'T GET BACK...APRIL, CASEY... THEY **NEED** US.
A PERSON LIKE THIS, SOME KIND OF CRAZY LONER IN A CAVE, HE DOESN'T UNDERSTAND WHAT THAT SENSE OF **FAMILY** EVEN MEANS.

I DON'T THINK THAT'S FAIR.
I DON'T CARE ABOUT BEING FAIR! THIS GUY IS JUST--
JUST **WHAT,** EXACTLY?

CRUNCH

I THINK OUR ILLUSTRIOUS HOST HAS ARRIVED...

HOW DID YOU GET INTO THIS CAVE?
ACTUALLY, THE DEFENSES WEREN'T ALL THAT TOUGH ON THE SOUTH-EAST ENTRANCE TO THIS CAVE SYSTEM ABOUT SIX HUNDRED FEET DOWN AND A MILE OUT, I HAD THIS LITTLE FELLA--

OKAY, I GET THE SENSE YOU'RE NOT ENTIRELY IN THE MOOD FOR CONSTRUCTIVE CRITICISM RIGHT NOW.
I NEED ANSWERS. NOW. TO EVERY-THING.

YOU ARE PLAYING A GAME OF DECEPTION, BRUCE WAYNE.
HOW--
YOU KNOW MUCH MORE THAN YOU PRETEND, AND YOU ATTEMPT TO TRICK US INTO REVEALING MORE, SHOWING OUR HAND.
SUCH TRICKS ARE NOT NECESSARY. TELL US WHAT YOU KNOW.

I KNOW WHAT'S IMPORTANT. YOU ARE FROM ANOTHER WORLD. YOU FOLLOW THE WAY OF THE NINJA. BUT THAT DOESN'T EXPLAIN HOW YOU'VE LEARNED MY IDENTITY...
YOU HAVE DEDUCED MUCH ABOUT US, BUT DO NOT UNDERESTIMATE THIS OLD RAT'S SKILL.
I AM QUITE CAPABLE OF TRAILING A MAN IN A BATSUIT BACK TO HIS COMPANY LABORATORY UNNOTICED.
MY NAME IS SPLINTER. YOU HAVE MET MY SONS...LEONARDO, DONATELLO, MICHELANGELO, AND RAPHAEL.
YES. AND WORST OF ALL, THEIR LEADER. THE SHREDDER.
WE WERE IN THE MIDST OF A DEADLY BATTLE DEEP UNDER THE HEART OF OUR NEW YORK CITY...
THE BATTLE WAS DIFFICULT, AND WE WERE ON THE EDGE OF VICTORY, WHEN A TRANS-DIMENSIONAL BEING KNOWN AS KRANG--AN ENEMY OF BOTH OURSELVES AND THE FOOT CLAN--TELEPORTED US AWAY SO THAT HE WOULD FACE NO FURTHER OPPOSITION TO HIS GOALS FOR OUR WORLD.
WE EMERGED HERE, IN THE GOTHAM OF THIS WORLD, WHERE WE DISCOVERED THE SHREDDER'S PLANS...
...HE HAD FOUND A SCIENTIST WHO MIGHT BE ABLE TO BRING HIM HOME, GIVING HIM THE CHANCE TO OVERCOME KRANG, AND FINALLY TAKE THE POWER HE HAS ALWAYS BELIEVED HE SHOULD HAVE.
BUT IN DOING SO, HE PLANS ON STRANDING US HERE...
AND YOU KNOW WHAT THAT WILL MEAN.
THE MUTAGEN IN OUR BLOOD WILL BECOME INERT. WE WILL REVERT TO BASE ANIMALS, AND LOSE OURSELVES FOREVER.
RRRRRREEEEE

WE ARE FROM ANOTHER WORLD, SIMILAR TO YOURS IN MANY WAYS, BUT ALSO QUITE DIFFERENT. PART OF THE STORY YOU MAY FIND FAMILIAR...
THERE IS A DARKNESS, BATMAN, AN UNDERCURRENT OF MADNESS AND DANGER THAT EATS AWAY AT THE GOOD PEOPLE OF OUR CITY.
THIS DARKNESS HAS A NAME.
THE FOOT CLAN.
EEEEEEEEE
SIR, I'VE ACTIVATED THE CAVE'S FULL DEFENSES.
THEY WILL NOT BE ABLE TO ESCAPE.

OH, MAN...YOU'VE GOT A ROBOT DINOSAUR, AND A ROBOT BRITISH DUDE?
I ASSURE YOU, WHILE I AM NOT A ROBOT, I HAVE A PARTICULARLY GOOD RECIPE UPSTAIRS FOR TURTLE STEW.
ALFRED, STAND DOWN.
THANK YOU, BATMAN.
THESE ARE MY CHILDREN. MY FAMILY. WE NEED YOUR HELP TO FIND SHREDDER. WE NEED YOUR HELP TO GET HOME.
SO LIFELIKE...
WELL, I HOPE YOU'VE PACKED ALREADY.
BECAUSE I BELIEVE SHREDDER'S MACHINE IS READY TO GO ONLINE ANY MINUTE NOW.
WE WILL GET YOU HOME. TONIGHT.
SEE, MAN! I TOLD YOU HE WAS FREAKING AWESOME.
YEAH, WELL.
WE'LL SEE ABOUT THAT.

ceberg Lounge.
Now...
LEONARDO, IT'S NOT ENOUGH TO SUBDUE THE SOLDIERS. WE NEED SHREDDER. WE CAN'T LET HIM ESCAPE.
YES, SIR!
WHAT'D I TELL YOU, RAPH? WE'RE KICKING BUTT.
FOCUS, MIKEY.
SIR? REALLY.
SHUT UP, RAPH.
SHREDDER! FACE US!
YEAH, MAN. WHAT IS IT--ALREADY FIGURED OUT YOU'VE LOST OR SOMETHING?
I HAVEN'T LOST.
NOT TO SPLIT HAIRS, BUT I'M PRETTY SURE THIS IS EXACTLY WHAT LOSING LOOKS LIKE.
YOU'RE GOING HOME TONIGHT, THROUGH THAT GATE, IN HANDCUFFS.
NO, I'M NOT.

THE PORTAL!
NO!! NO!!!!!
DON'T WORRY... DOCTOR KHAN IS SAFE, WE CAN REBUILD IT.
ARE YOU SO CERTAIN?
BATMAN... THIS...THIS IS PENNY-ONE.
DOCTOR KHAN'S HEAD JUST...THERE MUST HAVE BEEN A SUBDERMAL BOMB IMPLANTED...
I'M
I PRESUME THAT'S YOUR ASSOCIATE OUTSIDE, TELLING YOU THAT THE ONLY MAN CAPABLE OF REBUILDING THE MACHINE IS DEAD.
THE WAY THE PEOPLE OF THIS CITY FEAR YOU, I EXPECTED MORE, BATMAN.

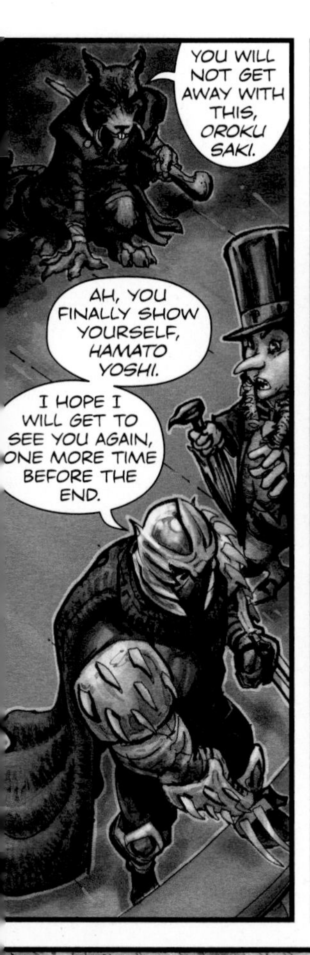
YOU WILL NOT GET AWAY WITH THIS, OROKU SAKI.
AH, YOU FINALLY SHOW YOURSELF, HAMATO YOSHI.
I HOPE I WILL GET TO SEE YOU AGAIN, ONE MORE TIME BEFORE THE END.

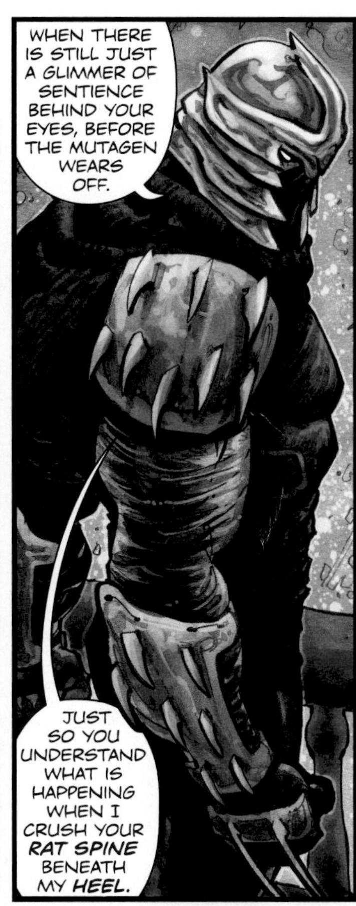
WHEN THERE IS STILL JUST A GLIMMER OF SENTIENCE BEHIND YOUR EYES, BEFORE THE MUTAGEN WEARS OFF.
JUST SO YOU UNDERSTAND WHAT IS HAPPENING WHEN I CRUSH YOUR RAT SPINE BENEATH MY HEEL.

YOU CAN'T DO THIS!
RAPH! NO!

GOODBYE.
NO!
HE NICKED AN ARTERY. WE'RE GOING TO NEED TO CLOSE IT UP.
BATMAN! WE NEED TO GET HIM BACK TO THE BATCAVE, NOW.
OH, MAN, OH, MAN...THIS IS BAD.
HE'S GOING TO BE OKAY, MIKEY. WE'VE STITCHED HIM UP FROM WORSE BEFORE.
NO, MAN... I MEAN THE DANG MACHINE JUST BLEW UP! ARE WE GOING TO BE ABLE TO GET **HOME?**
I DON'T KNOW, MIKEY...
DOES IT MEAN WE'RE GOING TO **DIE?**

OUR NUMBERS ARE DEPLETED, BUT IT'S NO MATTER. WE WILL BUILD AGAIN. THERE IS NO GOING HOME NOW.
ALL THAT'S LEFT IS BUILDING AN EMPIRE, HERE.

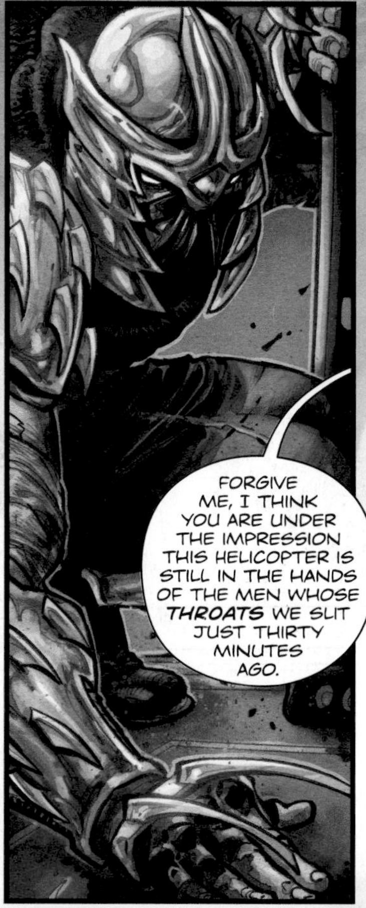
FORGIVE ME, I THINK YOU ARE UNDER THE IMPRESSION THIS HELICOPTER IS STILL IN THE HANDS OF THE MEN WHOSE ***THROATS*** WE SLIT JUST THIRTY MINUTES AGO.

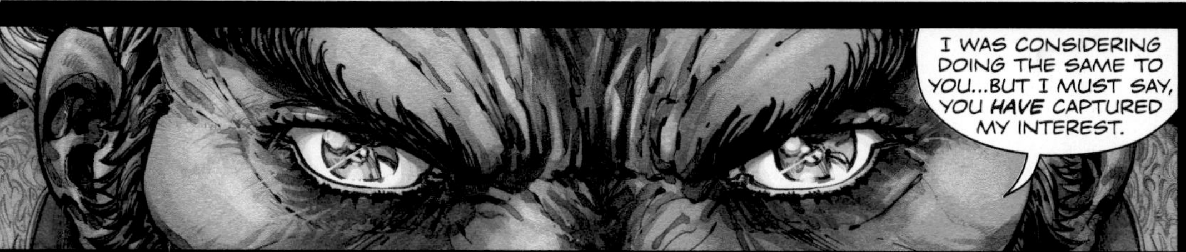
I WAS CONSIDERING DOING THE SAME TO YOU...BUT I MUST SAY, YOU ***HAVE*** CAPTURED MY INTEREST.

WHO ARE YOU?
YOUR NEW PARTNER.
YOU MAY CALL ME... RA'S AL GHUL!

WHAT IS YOUR NAME, SIR?
I AM OF ***THE FOOT.*** I HAVE NO NAME.

SIGH I'VE BEEN DOING THIS ALL DAY, I WOULD REALLY PREFER IF ONE OF YOU JUST GAVE ME A NAME.
I AM OF THE--
YEAH, YEAH. I'VE GOT IT.

KEEP HIM AS FAR FROM THE OTHER MEMBERS OF THIS "FOOT CLAN" AS POSSIBLE. I DON'T WANT THEM TO BE ABLE TO TALK TO EACH OTHER.

I SHOULD HAVE ***GORDON*** COMMITTED FOR SENDING IN OVER TWENTY OF THESE MANIACS. I DON'T LIKE ANY OF THIS.

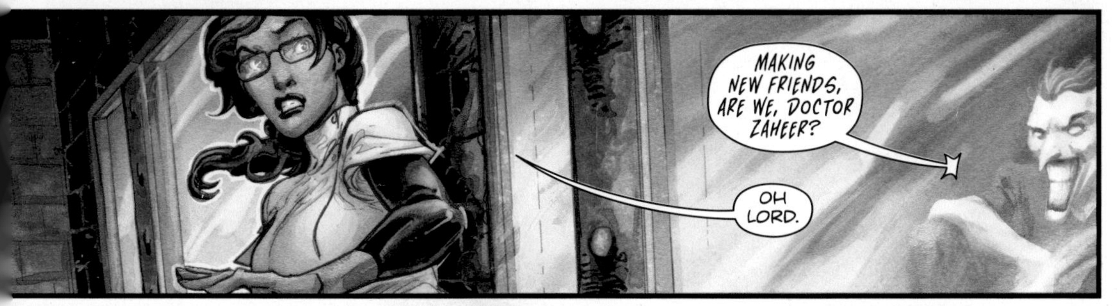
MAKING NEW FRIENDS, ARE WE, DOCTOR ZAHEER?
OH LORD.

YOU CAN'T KEEP SECRETS FROM ME... I CAN TELL SOMETHING FUN IS GOING ON OUT THERE, AND I WANT IN.
YOU DON'T REALLY EXPECT ME TO MISS OUT ON ALL OF THIS, NOW, DO YOU?
OPEN THE DOOR, AND WE CAN BRAID EACH OTHER'S HAIR, TELL SOME SECRETS SO I'M READY FOR THE BIG PARTY, MAYBE I'LL KILL A GUARD OR TWO IF I'M FEELING FESTIVE.

WHAT IS IT, DOCTOR ZAHEER?
DOUBLE HIS MEDICATION. RIGHT NOW.

THIS IS ALL BAD NEWS. I CAN FEEL IT.

OH MAHREEN, DON'T BE CROSS...
THE PARTY HASN'T EVEN **STARTED** YET!

ALL RIGHT, THAT SHOULD BE EVERYTHING...
YOU GOT A HANDLE ON ALL THOSE BOXES, MISTER?
YOUNG MAN, I ONCE SPENT SIX MONTHS WORKING AT ONE OF THE MOST EXCLUSIVE FIVE-STAR RESTAURANTS IN LONDON.
I THINK YOU'LL FIND I AM MORE THAN CAPABLE OF CARRYING A FEW PIZZAS.

PIZZA, I MEAN, REALLY...I OFFER TO MAKE A FEAST, AND THEY ASK FOR PIZZA...
SIGH TEENAGERS.
PIZZA WICK
RATTLE

WHAT ON EARTH...
RATTLE

ALL RIGHT, PERFECT SCORE SO FAR... AND NOW FOR THE FINAL TRICK...
NO.
WICK

COWABUNGA!!!
PIZZA
PIZZA WICK
PIZZA WICK
PIZZA WICK
PIZZA
PIZZA

OH, MAN! I'M SO SORRY, DUDE. ARE YOU OKAY?

MMMH, IT'S STILL GOOEY.
"FOCUS, MY SON...

HIS COSTUME IS DESIGNED TO INTIMIDATE YOU, BUT HE IS JUST A MAN. DO NOT LET HIM GET THE UPPER HAND.

WATCH YOUR FOOTWORK, HE IS PUSHING YOU FURTHER THAN YOU THINK.

HIS FOOTWORK LOOKS JUST FINE TO ME.
I WAS NOT SPEAKING TO LEONARDO, BATMAN.

I WAS **DISTRACTED.**
YEAH. KEEP TELLING YOURSELF THAT.

I STILL CAN'T GET OVER HOW AMAZING ALL OF THIS IS. FULL-ON 3-D HOLO-RECORDINGS OUT OF YOUR COWL FROM ALL YOUR MISSIONS?
I WANT COPIES OF ALL THE ONES FROM THE LAST FEW NIGHTS...

LOOK, THERE I AM, KNOCKING THAT DUMB LITTLE GUY'S HAT OFF!

AND THERE I GO AGAIN. THIS IS PRICELESS.
IT IS GOOD TO TAKE A MOMENT OF PLEASURE IN YOUR VICTORIES, BUT DO NOT LOSE THE LARGER PURPOSE.

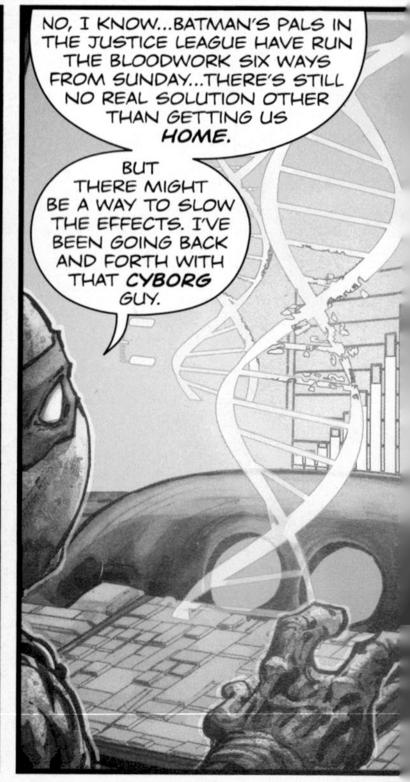
NO, I KNOW...BATMAN'S PALS IN THE JUSTICE LEAGUE HAVE RUN THE BLOODWORK SIX WAYS FROM SUNDAY...THERE'S STILL NO REAL SOLUTION OTHER THAN GETTING US **HOME.**
BUT THERE MIGHT BE A WAY TO SLOW THE EFFECTS. I'VE BEEN GOING BACK AND FORTH WITH THAT **CYBORG** GUY.

AND SHREDDER?
COMPLETELY AWOL...IT'S LIKE HE'S WAITING FOR SOMETHING...I JUST WISH WE KNEW WHAT...
NO, YOUNG MAN. I AM **KEEPING** THE SKATEBOARD UNTIL YOU LEARN NOT TO USE IT IN THE HOUSE.
DUUUUUDE! COME ON!

ALLING ME "DUDE" IS NOT HELPING YOUR SE, YOUNG MASTER MICHELANGELO.
COME ON, **OLD MASTER ALFRED!**
SIGH THAT IS **NOT** HOW THAT WORKS.
PIZZA WICK

I MIGHT NOT EVEN **KNOW** HOW TO RIDE A SKATEBOARD IN A FEW WEEKS! WOULD YOU ROB ME OF MY SIMPLE PLEASURES?
PIZZA WICK
YES. I CERTAINLY WILL.
AND HERE IS YOUR GREASY CHEESE BREAD.

THANK YOU FOR EVERYTHING, ALFRED.
WELL, COME ON, BATMAN. DIG IN.
I'M FINE.

DUDE. YOU ARE NOT FINE UNLESS YOU HAVE A DELICIOUS, GOOEY PIECE OF PEPPERONI PIZZA.
IT IS A DELICACY THAT BRIDGES ALL MEN, TURTLE **AND** BAT.

I'M CERTAINLY NOT THE ONE CLEANING THE GREASE OFF YOUR SUIT, I'LL SAY THAT MUCH.
IT'S GOOD.
REALLY.
THIS IS WHAT WE'RE DOING NOW?
WE'RE EATING PIZZA, AND GOING ON LITTLE DINKY ADVENTURES... YOU KNOW WHAT? I'M DONE.
YOU'RE OVER THE LINE, RAPH.
YEAH, MAN. THIS ISN'T COOL.
ISN'T COOL?! ISN'T COOL?!?!
WE'RE DYING! DID THAT ALL JUST SLIP OUT FROM YOUR MINDS?!
I CAN'T FREAKING STAND THIS.

IN A FEW DAYS WE'RE JUST GOING TO BE A FEW TURTLES AND A RAT THIS FREAKSHOW PUTS IN A CAGE OVER IN THE CORNER.
AND WE'RE HAVING A PIZZA PARTY? ARE YOU KIDDING ME?!
DON'T BRING PIZZA INTO THIS, DUDE.
RAPHAEL, WE'RE DOING EVERYTHING WE CAN...
OH, STOP PRETENDING HE'S NOT THE WHOLE REASON WE'RE IN THIS MESS. I SEE RIGHT THROUGH YOUR DUMB CAPE AND COWL, BATMAN
YOU WANT TO KNOW WHAT YOU ARE? YOU'RE JUST A THRILL-SEEKER. YOU'RE SOME RICH GUY WHO PUTS ON A COSTUME AND PUNCHES BAD GUYS BECAUSE IT SEEMS LIKE FUN.
YOU CHOSE THIS LIFE. WE DIDN'T. WE BECAME WHAT WE NEEDED TO BECOME TO SURVIVE. WE FIGHT SHREDDER BECAUSE IF WE DIDN'T, HE'D HAVE US ALL KILLED IN OUR SLEEP. BUT YOU DON'T CARE ABOUT ANY OF THAT, DO YOU?
THAT'S WHY WE FAILED. IF WE HADN'T LISTENED TO YOU, WE COULD HAVE SNUCK INTO THAT BASE AND GOTTEN HOME BY NOW. SHUT THE WHOLE THING DOWN FROM THE OTHER SIDE.
WE WOULDN'T BE STUCK HERE. WE WOULDN'T HAVE THIS DEATH SENTENCE OVER OUR HEADS. AND FOR SOME IDIOTIC REASON, THEY DON'T SEE THAT.
THEY THINK YOU'RE THE HERO YOU PRETEND TO BE.
BUT I SEE THE TRUTH. I SEE A SELFISH LITTLE RICH KID DOING ALL OF THIS FOR KICKS, AND THAT'S NOT SOMEONE I'M GOING TO PUT MY FAITH IN.
I'M NOT SPENDING ANOTHER DAMN MINUTE IN THIS CAVE. I'M DONE. COUNT ME OUT. I'M GOING TO GO ACTUALLY WORK ON SAVING OUR LIVES.
I'M GETTING US HOME.

THIS PLAN OF YOURS BETTER WORK, SHREDDER. I'M GROWING IMPATIENT.
IT WILL WORK.
DOCTOR KHAN NOTICED AN ANOMALY WHILE PINPOINTING THE FREQUENCY OF MY HOME DIMENSION...
...A TRANSMISSION FROM MY WORLD TO YOURS, AN OBJECT HURTLING BETWEEN WORLDS...
UNTIL I KNEW FOR CERTAIN THE SHAPE AND CONTENT OF THE TRANSMISSION, I WOULDN'T ALLOW IT TO BE DIRECTED. BUT YOUR SCIENTISTS WERE ABLE TO SHOW ME WHAT WAS COMING, AND NOW WE CAN BRING IT HERE.
AND WHAT *IS* COMING?
THE AMMUNITION WE NEED TO BURN GOTHAM TO THE GROUND.
ACTIVATE THE MACHINE.

PROCEED CAREFULLY. HE MAY BE DANGEROUS.
WHO MAY BE DANGEROUS?

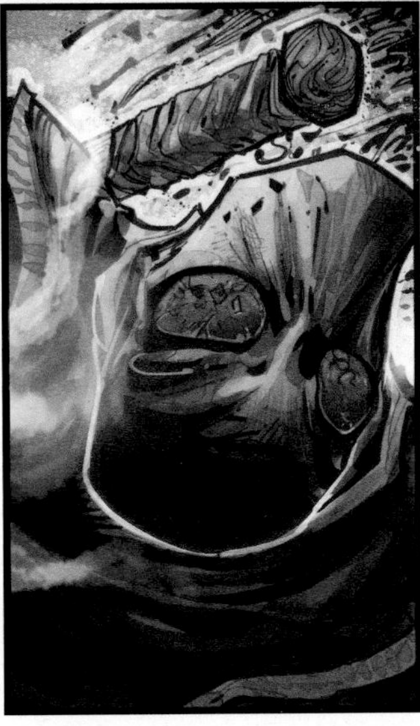

THE NAME'S CASEY JONES.
I JUST JUMPED THROUGH THE MULTIVERSE TO SAVE MY PALS, SO IF YOU THINK A FEW NINJAS ARE GOING TO SCARE ME OFF...
YOU CHUMPS HAVE ANOTHER THING COMIN'.

GET IN.
NAW, MAN. I'M DONE WITH ALL YOUR B.S.
RAPHAEL. I WANT YOU TO UNDERSTAND SOMETHING ABOUT ME. AFTER THAT, WE CAN GO OUR SEPARATE WAYS.

I WON'T EVEN TELL YOUR BROTHERS I SPOKE TO YOU.
BUT PLEASE. GET IN.

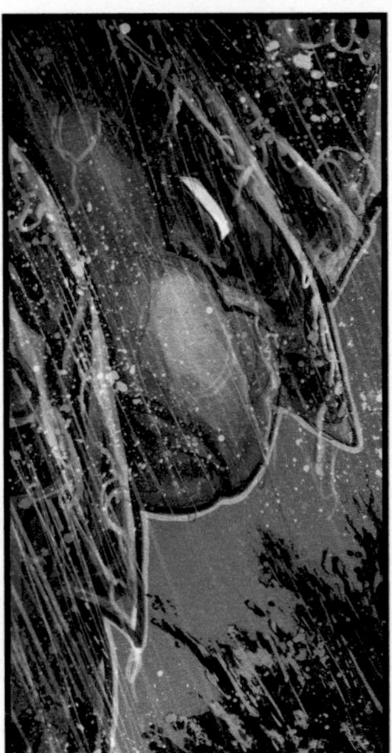

BETTER THAN THE RAIN, ANYWAYS. CAN'T YOU LIVE CLOSER TO GOTHAM? I MEAN, SERIOUSLY.

OH GOD! WHAT'S HAPPENING? DID I BREAK SOMETHING?
DID YOU SET AN ALARM ON SOME KIND OF ENERGY SIGNAL?
YEAH...THE SAME KIND OF TRANSDIMENSIONAL ENERGY BATMAN WAS ABLE TO PICK UP OFF OF OUR WEAPONS.
ALERT
ALERT

THERE'S A MASSIVE INFLUX OF ENERGY FLOWING INTO A WAREHOUSE IN THE NARROWS.

WE'RE GOING TO NEED TO GET INTO THE CITY FAST.
MASTER BRUCE HAS ALREADY TAKEN THE BATMOBILE...

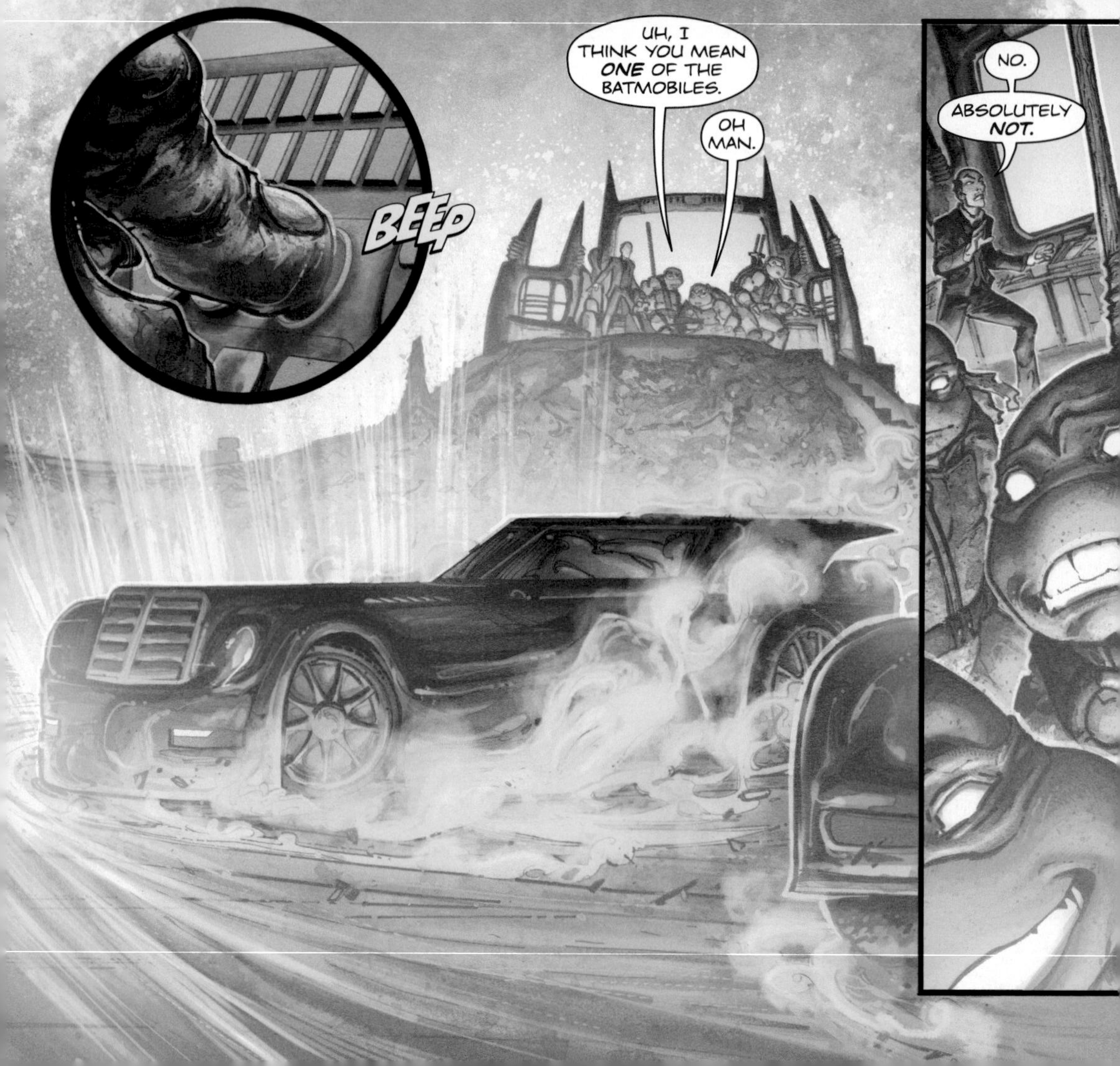
BEEP
UH, I THINK YOU MEAN ***ONE*** OF THE BATMOBILES.
OH MAN.
NO.
ABSOLUTELY ***NOT.***

WHAT IS THIS PLACE...
CRIME ALLEY.
CREATIVE FOLKS YOU'VE GOT HERE IN GOTHAM...
THIS IS WHERE I WATCHED MY PARENTS DIE, RAPHAEL.
THEY WERE KILLED BY AN ORDINARY MAN, A DOWN ON HIS LUCK THIEF WITH A GUN.
SHOT RIGHT IN FRONT OF ME FOR NO REASON OTHER THAN THE MONEY IN MY FATHER'S WALLET, AND THE PEARLS AROUND MY MOTHER'S NECK.
I WAS EIGHT YEARS OLD.

I'M...I'M SO SORRY.
I DIDN'T TAKE YOU HERE TO GUILT YOU. I WANT YOU TO UNDERSTAND.

THE WORST THING IMAGINABLE HAPPENED RIGHT IN FRONT OF MY EYES WHEN I WAS JUST A CHILD, AND ALL THE RULES OF THE WORLD WERE BROKEN. IT TOOK ME DECADES TO PULL MYSELF TOGETHER INTO SOMETHING NEW...SOMETHING STRONG.
A MAN WHO COULD OVERCOME WHAT HAD HAPPENED TO HIM, BUT ALSO A MAN WHO COULD WORK TIRELESSLY TO MAKE SURE THAT WHAT HAPPENED TO HIM WOULD NEVER HAPPEN TO ANOTHER FAMILY.
IT IS SELFISH, IN A WAY. I'LL GRANT YOU THAT. BUT IT'S WHAT I CAN DO. AND I NEED TO DO **SOMETHING.** I NEED TO DO IT FOR THEM.

HERE I STAND, AND I SEE A FAMILY BEING RIPPED APART BY IMPOSSIBLE SCIENCE AND DARK INTENT. I ***WON'T*** LET IT HAPPEN. I ***CAN'T*** LET IT.
SO PLEASE, HELP ME SAVE YOU AND YOUR FAMILY.

SIR...YOUNG MASTER DONATELLO PICKED UP A TRANSDIMENSIONAL READING IN THE CITY... THE TURTLES ARE EN ROUTE NOW...
I'M NOT SURE YOU'LL BE ENTIRELY THRILLED WITH THEIR MODE OF TRANSPORTATION.

COME ON, RAPHAEL.
WE HAVE WORK TO DO.

I GUESS WE DO.

OH GOD. BATMAN IS GOING TO KILL ME.
CASEY?! CASEY IS THAT YOU?!

YOU GUYS. IT'S CASEY!
IT'S SO GOOD TO SEE A FRIENDLY FACE, MAN.
YEAH, WELL, YOU'RE NOT GOING TO LIKE WHAT JUST HAPPENED...

SHREDDER AND THIS WEIRD DUDE WITH A GREEN CAPE JUST NICKED WHAT I CAME ALL THIS WAY TO GET TO YOU...THE MUTAGEN THAT COULD KEEP YOU ALIVE.
FIVE CANNISTERS. THE PURE STUFF.
YOU WOULDN'T BELIEVE WHAT I HAD TO DO TO GET IT IN THE FIRST PLACE.

YOU'RE TELLING ME THAT SHREDDER HAS PURE MUTAGEN IN *THIS* WORLD?
DID HE SAY WHERE HE WAS TAKING IT?
I WAS FOCUSED ON SURVIVING, MAN... AND I BARELY DID THAT...
BUT I DID HEAR ONE WORD...

"DOES 'ARKHAM' MEAN ANYTHING TO YOU GUYS?"

JUST KEEP TELLING YOURSELF...
IT'S JUST A TUESDAY. THINGS CAN'T GET ANY WEIRDER ON A TUESDAY.
JIM. *TELL* ME WHAT'S HAPPENED.
I LONG FOR THE DAYS WHEN I HAD A SIMPLE ANSWER TO THAT QUESTION.
JUST TELL ME YOU DON'T HAVE ANY **MORE** HEADACHES TUCKED IN THOSE ***GAUNTLETS*** OF YOURS.
I GUESS THAT DEPENDS...

WE LOOK LIKE HEADACHES TO YOU?

JUST CLOSE YOUR EYES AND THINK ABOUT RETIREMENT.
SOMEWHERE WARM WHERE THE GIANT TURTLES DON'T TALK.
JIM... THEY'RE FRIENDS.

SO, THAT'S WHAT FRIENDS LOOK LIKE, DO THEY? BARBARA KEEPS TELLING ME I SHOULD MAKE A FEW. BUT I HAVE TO SAY, I THINK I MIGHT PASS.
WHAT'S HAPPENED?
IT'S ARKHAM.

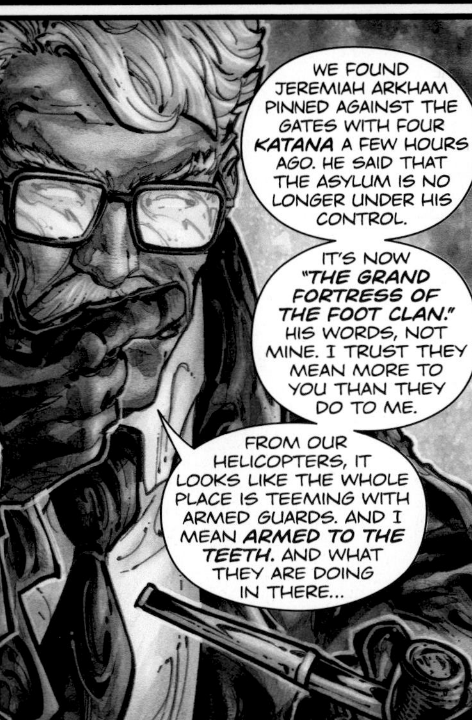
WE FOUND JEREMIAH ARKHAM PINNED AGAINST THE GATES WITH FOUR *KATANA* A FEW HOURS AGO. HE SAID THAT THE ASYLUM IS NO LONGER UNDER HIS CONTROL.
IT'S NOW ***"THE GRAND FORTRESS OF THE FOOT CLAN."*** HIS WORDS, NOT MINE. I TRUST THEY MEAN MORE TO YOU THAN THEY DO TO ME.
FROM OUR HELICOPTERS, IT LOOKS LIKE THE WHOLE PLACE IS TEEMING WITH ARMED GUARDS. AND I MEAN ***ARMED TO THE TEETH.*** AND WHAT THEY ARE DOING IN THERE...

LIKE I SAID. I LONG FOR THE DAYS...
...HEAR THE BIRD OUT YOURSELF.
THE SHREDDER IS BUILDING AN ARMY TO BURN GOTHAM CITY TO THE GROUND.
THE PROCESS HAS ALREADY BEGUN.
PENGUIN...

HE IS GOING TOO FAR, BATMAN. I NEVER SHOULD HAVE LET HIM IN.
HE'S TAKEN EVERYTHING FROM ME, AND I GUARANTEE YOU DO NOT WANT TO FACE WHAT HE CAN DO WITH MY RESOURCES.

WHY SHOULD WE LISTEN TO YOU?
TRUST ME, BOY, I DO NOT FIND THIS REMOTELY AMUSING... AND MY PATIENCE HAS WORN VERY THIN.
I AM PUTTING MYSELF ON THE LINE BY LYING TO SHREDDER LIKE THIS. IF HE SUSPECTS ANYTHING, THERE'S NO TELLING WHAT HE'LL DO TO ME.
YEAH, AND I'M SURE YOU DIDN'T MAKE ANY KIND OF DEAL TO MAKE SURE YOU'RE OFF THE HOOK FOR WHAT SHREDDER'S BEEN GETTING UP TO

DO NOT GIVE ME A REASON TO INCRIMINATE MYSELF IN FRONT OF THE COMMISSIONER. I'M HERE TO HELP YOU STOP THIS MANIAC AND HIS NEW PARTNER.

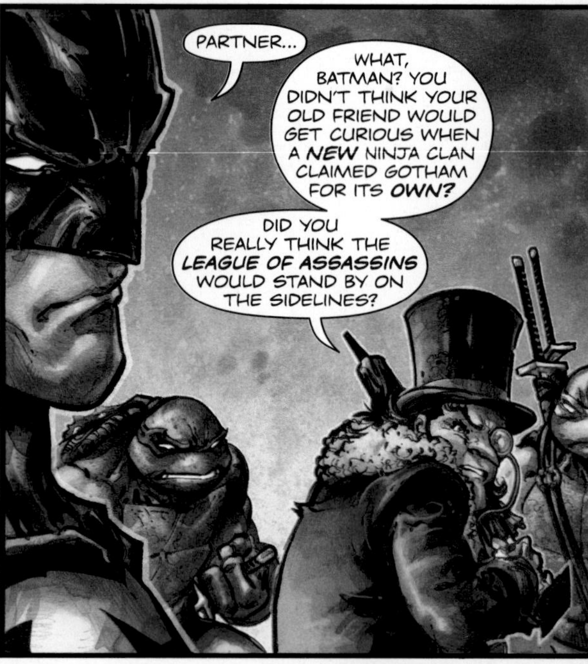
PARTNER...
WHAT, BATMAN? YOU DIDN'T THINK YOUR OLD FRIEND WOULD GET CURIOUS WHEN A NEW NINJA CLAN CLAIMED GOTHAM FOR ITS OWN?
DID YOU REALLY THINK THE LEAGUE OF ASSASSINS WOULD STAND BY ON THE SIDELINES?

RA'S AL GHUL.
BATMAN, WE HAVE THE FACILITY SURROUNDED, BUT I CAN'T SEE ANY WAY THROUGH WITHOUT MASSIVE CASUALTIES. WE'RE HOLDING THE FRONT, BUT THAT'S ABOUT ALL WE CAN DO FOR NOW.
CAN YOU HELP US?

THE CAR IS EN ROUTE. WE NEED TO GET THE OTHERS FAST, AND GET TO ARKHAM.
BATMAN...WHO IS THIS GUY...THIS RAY...RACIAL GHOUL?
RA'S AL GHUL...
HE'S ONE OF THE MOST DANGEROUS MEN ON THE PLANET.
BUT SO AM I.
WAIT... THINK I NEED TO...
AUGH!
LEO, WHAT'S WRONG?!
IT'S STARTING... THE MUTAGEN IS WEARING OFF...
OH, NO...

"...WE'RE RUNNING OUT OF TIME."
C'MON... C'MON...JUST A LITTLE MORE...

YEAH! IN YOUR FACE!!
WINNER
2nd Player
YEAH, YEAH.
PIZZA THE FOURTH

MY PONY RACERS WILL CONQUER THE UNIVERSE!!

SO, THIS IS WHAT YOU'VE BEEN GETTING UP TO, HUH?
I RUSH TO ANOTHER FREAKING UNIVERSE TO SAVE YOU PUNKS AND YOU'RE ALL PLAYING VIDEO GAMES.

IN A WEIRD CAVE WITH A DINOSAUR.
I KNOW, RIGHT?! IT'S AMAZING!

CASEY, YOU SHOULD BE LYING DOWN. THAT FIGHT TOOK A LOT OUT OF YOU.
I'VE RESTED LONG ENOUGH...IT'S TIME FOR US TO GET *MOVING.*
HAROLD EXPLAINED WHAT WAS HAPPENING TO YOU GUYS. I DON'T THINK YOU KNOW HOW SERIOUS IT IS. WHERE ARE THE OTHERS?
d Player

THEY ARE OUT ON SECRET BATMAN MISSIONS. DOING SECRET BATMAN THINGS.

WE STAYED BEHIND TO KEEP AN EYE ON YOU. YOU KNOW YOU PASSED OUT IN THE BATMOBILE?
NEEDED MY *BEAUTY SLEEP,* MIKEY.
BUT WE NEED TO ROUND THE GANG UP. SERIOUSLY. THIS IS IMPORTANT.

I'LL BE THE ONE DECIDING WHAT'S IMPORTANT FROM HERE ON OUT.

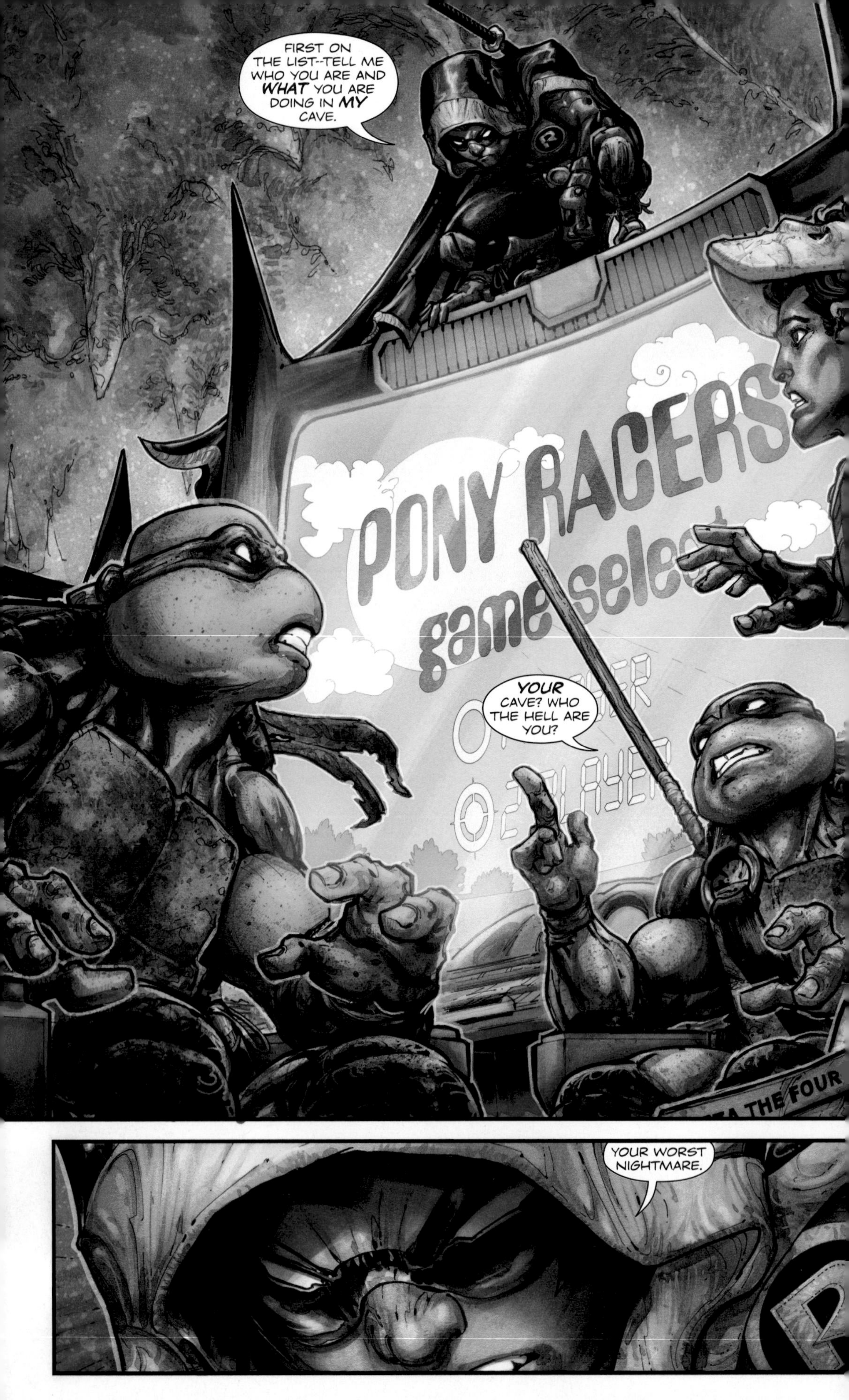
FIRST ON THE LIST--TELL ME WHO YOU ARE AND **WHAT** YOU ARE DOING IN **MY** CAVE.
PONY RACERS
YOUR CAVE? WHO THE HELL ARE YOU?
YOUR WORST NIGHTMARE.

HAH.

WHAT ARE YOU, FIVE YEARS OLD?
HH.

PIZZA THE FOURTH
WHAT THE--

YOU DON'T WANT TO DO THIS, KID.
TT

OH, YES. I DO.

WHOK
WHUMP
OOF!
?!

DID YOU WIRE Y QBOX INTO THE BATCOMPUTER?!

YEAH! HOW COULD YOU NOT WANT TO PLAY ON THAT THING? HAVE YOU SEEN IT?
WHY WOULD THIEVES WANT TO PLAY VIDEO GAMES?
THAT'S WHAT WE'RE TELLING YOU, KID. WE ARE NOT THIEVES! WE'RE WITH BATMAN!

PROVE IT.
DAMIAN.

STAND DOWN.
LEO!
WHAT'S WRONG WITH HIM?

MASTER BRUCE, WE GOT YOUR MESSAGE. WHAT CAN WE DO?
I'M NOT SURE THERE'S ANYTHING WE **CAN** DO.
THIS IS JUST WHAT HAROLD SAID WOULD HAPPEN...
HAROLD?

HE'S A SCIENTIST BACK HOME, BEEN HELPING US FOR A WHILE.
HE'S THE WHOLE REASON I WAS ABLE TO MAKE THE TRIP HERE.
LEO'S BODY IS GOING INTO SHOCK...THE MUTAGEN IS **REVERTING...** IT'LL PASS NOW, BUT IT'S ONLY 24 HOURS UNTIL HIS MIND WILL PRETTY MUCH **SHUT DOWN.** AND IF IT'S HAPPENING TO HIM, IT'LL HAPPEN TO THE REST OF YOU VERY SOON.

LOOK, I KNOW YOU WANTED TO TRACK DOWN THE FOOT CLAN BEFORE WE PUT THIS BAD BOY TO WORK, BUT I THINK IT'S TIME TO GO **HOME.**
WHAT **IS** THAT?
I SHOWED THE TURTLES LAST NIGHT...IT'S HOW I GOT HERE. IT'S A **SLINGSHOT.**
I'M NOT GOING TO PRETEND TO KNOW HOW IT WORKS, BUT THAT'S HOW HE EXPLAINED IT.

THIS THING HAS BEEN BUILDING ENERGY AND IS STILL HOOKED INTO THE PORTAL DEVICE BACK HOME. IT'LL ONLY WORK **ONCE,** AND WE NEED TO USE IT FAST...
SOMETHING ABOUT **DIMENSIONAL POSITIONING** AND THE **AXIS OF THE EARTH** AND BLAH BLAH BLAH.
BUT BASICALLY, IF I GET THE RIGHT POWER BOOST, I CAN GET US ALL HOME, **NOW.**

IF WE DON'T GO BACK NOW, HAROLD SAID TO TELL YOU IT'LL BE **WEEKS** BEFORE WE COULD TRY ANOTHER MISSION...AND BY THEN...
YEAH, MAN. WE GET THE PICTURE.

WE... CAN'T...
SHREDDER.

NEED TO BRING **SHREDDER BACK...**
DUDE...NO, WE ***DON'T.*** WE LEAVE HIM HERE AND HE'LL NEVER BE ABLE TO BOTHER US AGAIN. WE CAN TAKE DOWN KRANG AND PUT OUR CITY RIGHT.
BUT WHAT HE'S DOING... PEOPLE ARE DYING...
ROBIN AND I CAN FACE HIM. WE'VE FACED WORSE BEFORE.
FATHER... I WISH TO SPEAK TO YOU IN PRIVATE.
DAMIAN, THERE ISN'T TIME FOR THAT.
FINE.

I'VE BEEN OVERSEAS TRACKING THE MOVEMENTS OF THE LEAGUE OF ASSASSINS...
...THEY ARE CONVERGING **HERE.** IN **GOTHAM.**
HOW LONG DO WE HAVE?
HOURS.

THEN WE NEED TO GET TO ARKHAM. **NOW.**

BATMAN.
DO NOT UNDERESTIMATE THE SHREDDER.

I WON'T.

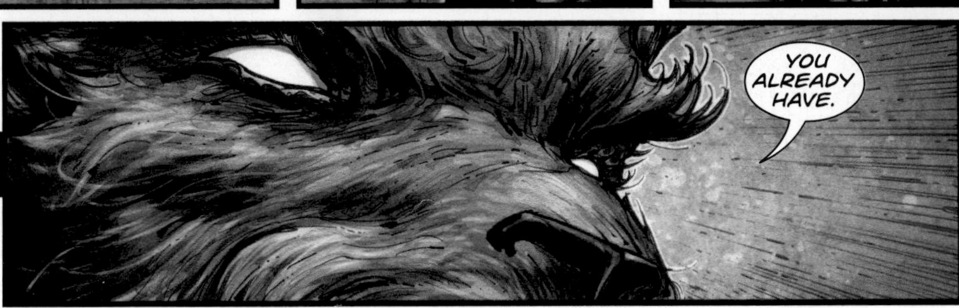
YOU ALREADY HAVE.

YOUR SON, HERE, HAS TOLD YOU OF A COMING ARMY. YOU BELIEVE THAT THIS RA'S AL GHUL PLOTS A DOUBLE-CROSS.
WHY ELSE WOULD HE BRING HIS FORCES HERE OTHER THAN TO TAKE DOWN SHREDDER AND REAP THE REWARDS OF HIS CONQUEST?
BUT YOU DON'T SEE THE DOUBLE-CROSS COMING FROM SHREDDER **HIMSELF**. YOU DON'T KNOW THE LENGTHS TO WHICH HE WILL GO IN ORDER TO WIN.

THANK YOU FOR YOUR GUIDANCE, MASTER SPLINTER.
BUT WE WILL **HANDLE** IT.

SIR. PERHAPS IT'S TIME TO DEBUT THE **INTIMIDATOR SUIT...**
WITH EVERYTHING THAT'S HAPPENED, I HAVEN'T HAD THE TIME TO **PERFECT** IT.
WE'LL BE FINE AS WE ARE. WE'VE GOT OUR FAIR SHARE OF EXPERIENCE FIGHTING **NINJA.**

IT WAS AN HONOR WORKING WITH YOU, BATMAN.
LIKEWISE.

AWW, MAN, IT CAN'T BE OVER ALREADY.
MIKEY...
FATHER. COME ON.

ALFRED. GIVE THEM ANYTHING THEY NEED. GET THEM HOME SAFE.
YES, SIR.

WHAT ABOUT THE CAR?
WE'RE NOT TAKING THE CAR.

INTERESTING FRIENDS YOU'VE BEEN MAKING.
FOCUS, ROBIN.

I'M SORRY I WASN'T ABLE TO STOP THE LEAGUE FROM EMBARKING...
YOU DON'T NEED TO BE SORRY. YOU BROUGHT THE INFORMATION HERE IN TIME. YOU DID WELL.

ALFRED CALLED...HE SAID THE ANNIVERSARY OF YOUR PARENTS' MURDER IS IN JUST A FEW DAYS. I HADN'T REALIZED. I HAD MEANT TO BE HOME...

YOU'RE HOME NOW.
AND WE HAVE WORK TO DO.

YOUR WORK WILL BE CUT OUT FOR YOU, BATMAN.
PENGUIN...

THE SHREDDER SAYS...IF I WAS SO EAGER TO GIVE HIS SECRETS TO THE ENEMY...I WOULD BE THE FIRST TO FACE HIS PROCESS...
AND THE ONE WHO WOULD HAVE TO FACE **YOU** FIRST.
IN MY NEW FORM.
PENGUIN, WHAT HAVE THEY DONE TO YOU...
HE SAYS THAT WITHIN THESE WALLS WERE MEN AND WOMEN WHO HAD BROUGHT THIS CITY TO THE EDGE OF RUIN COUNTLESS TIMES...
BATMAN, WE'RE NOT ALONE...
...BUT NOW...
...IT IS TIME TO PUSH THE CITY ***OVER THE EDGE.***

STARTING WITH YOU.

I DON'T CARE FOR YOUR VILLAINS' MAKEOVERS.
TAKE IT UP WITH YOUR GRANDFATHER.
Arkham Asylum.

I'VE NEVER FELT STRENGTH LIKE THIS...
YOU WON'T FEEL IT FOR LONG, BANE.

BUT THIS WILL LINGER A WHILE.

FZZZZAPP

ARRRHH!

C'MON, MR. B...WE JUST WANT TO HAVE A LITTLE FUN!

HE'LL PASS.

WE NEED TO FIND RA'S AND SHREDDER.

YOU'RE GOING TO PAY FOR WHAT THEY'VE DONE TO ME...

I COULD NOT CARE LESS ABOUT MY TRANSFORMATION.
BUT YOU HAVE OTHER SINS TO ACCOUNT FOR, BATMAN.

FOOOOOSH
UNNNH.

ALERT
BATMAN! THIS IS PENNY ONE! DO YOU COPY?

THEY'RE KILLING HIM...
I--I'M FEELING BETTER...A BIT WOOZY, BUT I'M FINE...
GUYS, YOU ARE **NOT** FINE. THE MUTAGEN INS OF YOU IS GOING IN YOU ARE GOING TO IF YOU STAY HER AND I DON'T KNO ***WHEN*** I'LL BE AB TO GET BACK TO YOU.
THINK ABOU EACH OTHER. T ABOUT US, B HOME.
THE MACHINE IS READY. WE HAVE TO GO NOW.
I DON'T LIKE THIS ONE BIT.
HEY, GUYS, HE'S A DANG SUPERHERO. HE'LL BE FINE. THINK OF ***LEO***.

LOOK, CASEY!
YOU'RE TALKING ABOUT A MAN WHO HAS SPENT THE LAST WEEK GIVING EVERYTHING HE HAS TO HELP US. A MAN WHO JUST WALKED INTO A ROOM FULL OF HIS WORST VILLAINS--VILLAINS POWERED WITH A DANGEROUS MUTAGEN FROM OUR WORLD, BY THE WAY. STUFF THAT'S ONLY HERE BECAUSE OF US.
NOW HE MIGHT DIE BECAUSE OF THE PROBLEMS WE LEFT BEHIND.

THINK ABOUT YOUR BROTHERS, RAPH. THINK ABOUT YOUR FAMILY.
I'M THINKING ABOUT THE MAN WHO TOLD ME THAT HE'S SPENT HIS ENTIRE LIFE PROTECTING FAMILIES LIKE OURS BECAUSE HE LOST HIS OWN.
THE TRANSPORTER IS FULLY POWERED. IT'S GOING TO ACTIVATE ANY SECOND NOW REGARDLESS OF WHAT YOU DECIDE, AND THEN I'M GONE WITH OR WITHOUT YOU. IT'S NOW OR NEVER...
WHAT ARE YOU GOING TO DO?

ROBIN. YOU KNOW WHAT TO DO...
I CAN'T LEAVE YOU LIKE THIS, FATHER.

WE CAN'T LE THEM LEAVE FACILITY. DO WORRY ABO ME. *GO. NO*

AND ROB THESE LOVELY MEN AND WOMEN OF THEIR CHANCE TO EXPLORE THEIR NEW ABILITIES? I WOULDN'T DREAM OF IT, BATMAN.

ALL ACCORDING TO OUR MACHINATIONS, BATMAN.
YOU CONTINUE TO UNDERESTIMATE ME, DETECTIVE. IT'S HARD TO BELIEVE I ONCE THOUGHT YOU HAD IT IN YOU TO REPLACE ME.
I AM NOT ABOVE COLLABORATION WHEN I FIND A LIKE-MINDED ALLY. I HAVE LIVED FOR HUNDREDS OF YEARS, I KNOW HOW TO PLAY ON A LARGER SCALE.
GOTHAM HAS SCARRED THE WORLD FOR TOO LONG. IT'S TIME TO REMOVE IT FROM THE PICTURE...

RA'S!
SHOW YOURSELF!
YOUR FIGHT'S WITH ME!
SHREDDER. HE'S DOUBLE-CROSSING YOU...
AN ARMY OF ASSASSINS IS EN ROUTE TO GOTHAM. HE'LL TAKE CONTROL. TAKE YOU OUT...

THE LEAGUE OF ASSASSINS AND THE FOOT CLAN LL RAIN OUR TERROR ON ERY MAJOR CITY AROUND HE GLOBE, USING THIS MAGNIFICENT MUTAGEN TO TRANSFORM EACH CITY'S ENEMIES INTO UNSTOPPABLE BEASTS OF NATURE.
AND THEN THE TRUE NATURAL ORDER OF THE WORLD WILL ASSERT ITSELF, AND WE WILL HOLD THE REINS.

I EXPECTED MORE OF A FIGHT OUT OF YOU, WARRIOR.

I SHARE YOUR ADVERSARY'S DISAPPOINTMENT. I HAD THOUGHT I MIGHT END YOUR PAIN MYSELF, BUT IT IS BENEATH ME.
BUT THERE'S ONE WHO IS EAGER TO TAKE THE JOB FOR HIMSELF.

SSSSMILE, BATSY.
I WONDER WHAT KIND OF VENOM IS RUNNING THROUGH THESE VEINS? I SURE HOPE I GIVES YOU A GRIN. I WOULDN' WANT YOU TO DIE WITH THAT ROTTEN SSSSCOWL ON YOUR FACE.
I KNEW YOU WOULDN'T LEAVE ME OUT OF ALL OF THE FUN. AFTER YOU, I'LL TAKE THE REST.

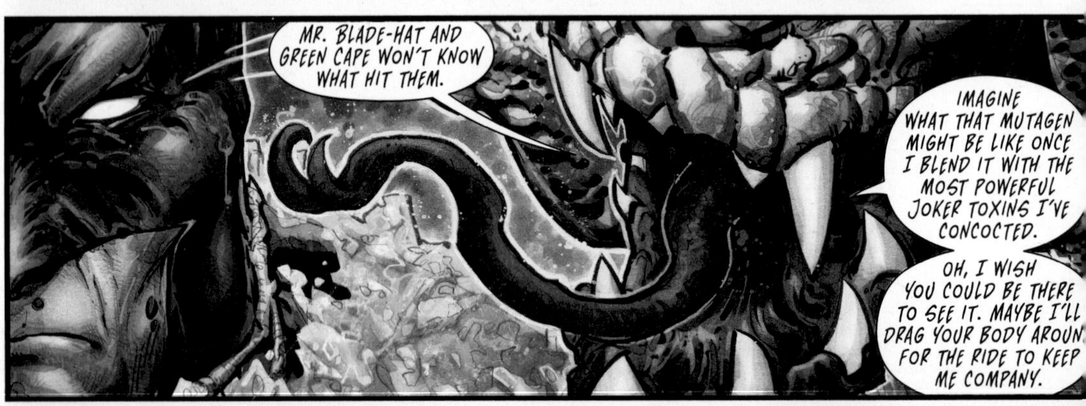
MR. BLADE-HAT AND GREEN CAPE WON'T KNOW WHAT HIT THEM.
IMAGINE WHAT THAT MUTAGEN MIGHT BE LIKE ONCE I BLEND IT WITH THE MOST POWERFUL JOKER TOXINS I'VE CONCOCTED.
OH, I WISH YOU COULD BE THERE TO SEE IT. MAYBE I'LL DRAG YOUR BODY AROUN FOR THE RIDE TO KEEP ME COMPANY.

MASTER SHREDDER, THE POLICE FORCES SURROUNDING THE ASYLUM HAVE TRIPLED.
OPEN THE GATES. IT'S TIME TO SHOW THIS CITY THE MEANING OF FEAR.

SORRY, SHRED-HEAD
WHUMPF

WE HAD MORE OF AN INTIMATE GATHERING IN MIND.
H-HOW... YOU SHOULD BE GONE...
WE COULDN'T LEAVE YOU BEHIND, BATMAN. THIS IS OUR MESS. WE'RE GOING TO CLEAN IT UP.
BUT THAT MEANS...
WE'LL FIGURE OUT WHAT THAT MEANS TOGETHER. YOU NEEDED US. WE'RE HERE. THAT'S WHAT MATTERS.
AND TRUST US, DUDE. WE KNOW HOW TO KICK SOME MUTANT BE-HINDS.
HERE, THIS SHOULD GET YOU OUT OF THERE.
NEED TO FACE SHREDDER...
I MIGHT BE ABLE TO HELP WITH THAT. WE BROUGHT SOMETHING ALONG FOR THE RIDE... BARELY FIT IN THE CAR...
I TINKERED WITH IT A BIT. I THINK YOU'LL BE PLEASANTLY SURPRISED.

RAPH! LOOK. IT'S A POLAR BEAR WITH AN ICE GUN! HOW FREAKING COOL IS THAT?
YOU WANT COOL, CHILD? I'LL GIVE YOU COOL.
AW, MAN. YOU'VE GOT THE LINES DOWN AND EVERYTHING. A-PLUS. GOOD JOB.
FOCUS, MIKEY!

HEY DUDE, YOU GOTTA GIVE CREDIT WHERE CREDIT'S DUE.

WHERE'S THAT WEIRD BIRD WITH THE PUPPET? GONNA HIT 'IM WI MY NUNCHUCKS

WE MUST NIP THIS IN THE BUD. THEY MUST DIE, AND QUICKLY.
I WHOLE-HEARTEDLY AGREE.

THAT WON'T BE HAPPENING.

THIS ENDS NOW.
YOU THINK THAT PATHETIC SUIT CAN DO YOUR FIGHTING FOR YOU?

NO. BUT IT **WILL** HURT.

AH, YES, THIS WILL DO NICELY.

YOU CAN'T FIGHT US BOTH, BATMAN.

HE DOESN'T HAVE TO.

HMPH! THE USUAL GAME.
BATMAN SENDS CHILDREN TO FIGHT HIS BATTLES.
IT'S TIME ANOTHER DIED TO SHOW HIM HIS FOLLY.
YIELD, BATMAN.
NEVER.
CRACK
RRRKKK

YOU THINK YOU ARE THE ONLY ONE WITH A TRICK UP HIS SLEEVE?
FOOOSH
BURN.

ANY LAST WORDS?
CLOSER...

THIS IS FUTILE.

YOU WANT TO LOOK ME IN THE EYES?
HE'S BLOCKING EVERY BLOW!
JUST KEEP POWERING THROUGH...

...FOR THIS.
WHOOM
NO. I WANT YOU IN THE RIGHT POSITION...
ATTACK HIM TOGETHER!
ALL RIGHT, THEN. NO MORE GAMES.

JUST BLOOD.

IT'S OVER, SHREDDER.
MY SOLDIERS...MY WEAPONS...
BRING HIM DOWN!
I AM AFRAID THEY ARE RESTING.
I RECOMMEND YOU FOLLOW SUIT.
N-NO...I WON'T LET THIS HAPPEN.
ASSASSINS. TAKE YOUR POSITIONS...I NEED YOU TO OVERWHELM THE ASYLUM NOW.

THAT WON'T BE HAPPENING, GRANDFATHER.
I DISARMED YOUR MEN, AND LED THE GCPD TO APPREHEND THEM. THIS BATTLE IS OVER.
WELL PLAYED, DAMIAN.

UNTIL THE NEXT GAME, THEN.

WHERE DID HE GO?
HE'LL BE OUT OF THE COUNTRY WITHIN 20 MINUTES. IT'S NOT WORTH THE RAT CHASE.
ER. NO OFFENSE.
NONE TAKEN, YOUNG MAN.

IT'S NICE TO SEE SHREDDER OUT COLD LIKE THAT. MAN, I WISH I COULD JUST--
NO, RAPHAEL.
YOU WILL TAKE HIM WITH YOU TO YOUR PRISON. YOU WILL HAVE HIM ANSWER FOR HIS CRIMES.
HOW TO GET HOME IS STILL A PRETTY BIG FREAKING ISSUE...

I THINK I MIGHT HAVE A SOLUTION ON THAT FRONT...
HEY, GUYS.
APRIL!
WHEN CASEY CAME BACK WITHOUT YOU, WE GOT RIGHT TO WORK. HAROLD AND I HAD BEEN WORKING TO KEEP A LOCK ON THE FREQUENCY OF THIS UNIVERSE, AND KNOWING THAT WE'D BE TRACING A HUGE AMOUNT OF ACTIVE MUTAGEN HELPED US PINPOINT THIS LOCATION.
HAROLD SAID THAT HIS PORTAL WOULD EITHER SEND US SPIRALING INTO AN ETERNAL ABYSS OF NEVER-ENDING PAIN AND TERROR, OR WE'D WIND UP RIGHT UP IN THE MIDDLE OF WHATEVER MESS YOU GUYS GOT YOURSELVES INTO.
WE DON'T HAVE LONG, THOUGH...HAROLD SAYS MAYBE TWENTY MINUTES UNTIL THE WHOLE SYSTEM SHORT-CIRCUITS.
Aw, MAN. I TOTALLY MISSED THE FIGHT, DIDN'T I?
TRUST ME, MAN! IT WAS WEIRD!
TWENTY MINUTES SHOULD BE ENOUGH TIME TO ROUND UP ALL OF THE FOOT CLAN AND SEND THEM THROUGH.
THANK YOU, BATMAN. FOR EVERYTHING.
NO...I OWE YOU MY LIFE. THANK YOU.

THANKS, ALL OF YOU.
YEAH, WE'RE PRETTY SWEET.

HEY, BATS...

THIS IS FOR YOU.

WHAT--
I KNOW YOU LOST YOUR FAMILY WAY BACK WHEN. BUT YOU'VE GOT A HELL OF A GOOD ONE **NOW.** I'M GLAD I GOT TO MEET YOU.
AND IF YOU EVER COME ROUND OUR PLACE...
...YOU HAVE ANOTHER.

Hours later.
OUR SCIENTISTS ARE BACKING UP YOUR CLAIMS. SEEMS LIKE THE WHOLE ZOO IS GOING TO TURN BACK TO NORMAL IN THE NEXT WEEK OR SO. WHATEVER ARKHAM NORMAL IS, AT LEAST.
A.R.G.U.S. JUST ARRIVED WITH A CREW THAT CAN KEEP THEM ALL IN LINE IN THE MEANTIME. I'M ALSO KEEPING BULLOCK ON-SITE FOR AT LEAST THE WEEKEND TO MAKE SURE NOTHING SLIPS PAST US.
SO IT LOOKS LIKE WE'RE SET.
THANK YOU, JIM.

IT'S OVER, THEN.
YES, IT IS. THE TURTLES SHOULD BE BACK HOME AND SAFE. GOTHAM WILL RETURN TO NORMAL.

I JUST REALIZED...IT'S DAWN. IT'S TODAY, ISN'T IT? THE ANNIVERSARY OF YOUR PARENTS' DEATH. I CAN LEAVE, FATHER... I KNOW YOU TYPICALLY CARE TO ENDURE THIS ALONE.
NO. I'D LIKE YOU TO STAY, DAMIAN.
PERHAPS WE COULD PUT ON SOME OLD FAMILY VIDEOS. SEE YOUNG MASTER BRUCE WADDLING AROUND IN HIS PRE-COSTUME DAYS.
HH.

THAT INTIMIDATOR SUIT...IT WAS IMPRESSIVE, BUT I SAW SOME KEY STRUCTURAL FLAWS.
PERHAPS WE COULD GO OVER THE SCHEMATICS. TOGETHER.

I'D LIKE THAT.

THE END... FOR NOW!

BATMAN/
TEENAGE MUTANT NINJA TURTLES
COVER GALLERY

BATMAN/TMNT #1 cover art by Freddie E Williams II

BATMAN/TMNT #1 variant cover art
by Kevin Eastman and Tomi Varga

BATMAN/TMNT #1
2nd printing cover art
by Freddie E Williams II

BATMAN/TMNT #1
3rd printing cover art
by Freddie E Williams II

BATMAN/TMNT #1 Fried Pie Comics variant cover art by Rafael Albuquerque

BATMAN/TMNT #1 Bulletproof Comics and Games variant cover art by Gabriele Dell'otto

BATMAN/TMNT #1 Bulletproof Comics and Games black-and-white variant cover art by Gabriele Dell'otto

BATMAN/TMNT #1 Captain's Comics and Toys variant cover art by Kenneth Rocafort

BATMAN/TMNT #1 Captain's Comics and Toys black-and-white variant cover art by Kenneth Rocafo

BATMAN/TMNT #1
Comickaze variant cover art
by Carlos D'Anda

BATMAN/TMNT #1 Comickaze black and white variant cover art by Carlos D'Anda

TMAN/TMNT #1 Conquest Comics
iant cover art by Stanley "Artgerm" Lau

BATMAN/TMNT #1 Conquest Comics hybrid variant cover art by Stanley "Artgerm" Lau

BATMAN/TMNT #1 Conquest Comics black-and-white variant cover art by Stanley "Artgerm" Lau

BATMAN/TMNT #1 Dynamic Forces
variant cover art by Neal Adams

BATMAN/TMNT #1 Dynamic Forces black-and-white variant cover art by Neal Adams

BATMAN/TMNT #1 Gamestop variant cover art by David Wilkins

BATMAN/TMNT #1
The Hall of Comics variant cover art
by Ivan Reis and Marcelo Maiolo

BATMAN/TMNT #1 Hastings variant cover art
by Tyler Kirkham and Tomeu Morey

BATMAN/TMNT #1 Hastings black-and-white variant cover art
by Tyler Kirkham and Tomeu Morey

BATMAN/TMNT #1 Amazing! Comic Conventions
variant cover art by Eddie Nunez

BATMAN/TMNT #1 Amazing! Comic Conventions
black-and-white variant cover art by Eddie Nunez

BATMAN/TMNT #1 Midtown Comics variant cover art by Cliff Chiang

BATMAN/TMNT #1 Midtown Comics black-and-white variant cover art by Cliff Chiang

BATMAN/TMNT #1 Newbury Comics variant
cover art by Michael Allred and Laura Allred

BATMAN/TMNT #1 Newbury Comics
black-and-white variant cover art by Michael Allred

BATMAN/TMNT #1 Planet Comics variant cover
art by Nick Dragotta and Lee Loughridge

BATMAN/TMNT #1 Planet Comics black-and-white variant cover art by Nick Dragotta

BATMAN/TMNT #1 Tate's Comics variant cover art
by Kevin Eastman and Tomi Varga

BATMAN/TMNT #2 cover art
by Freddie E Williams II

BATMAN/TMNT #2 variant cover art by Kevin Eastman and Tomi Varga

BATMAN/TMNT #2 2nd printing
cover art by Freddie E Williams II

BATMAN/TMNT #2 3rd printing
cover art by Freddie E Williams II

BATMAN/TMNT #2 4th printing cover art by Freddie E Williams II

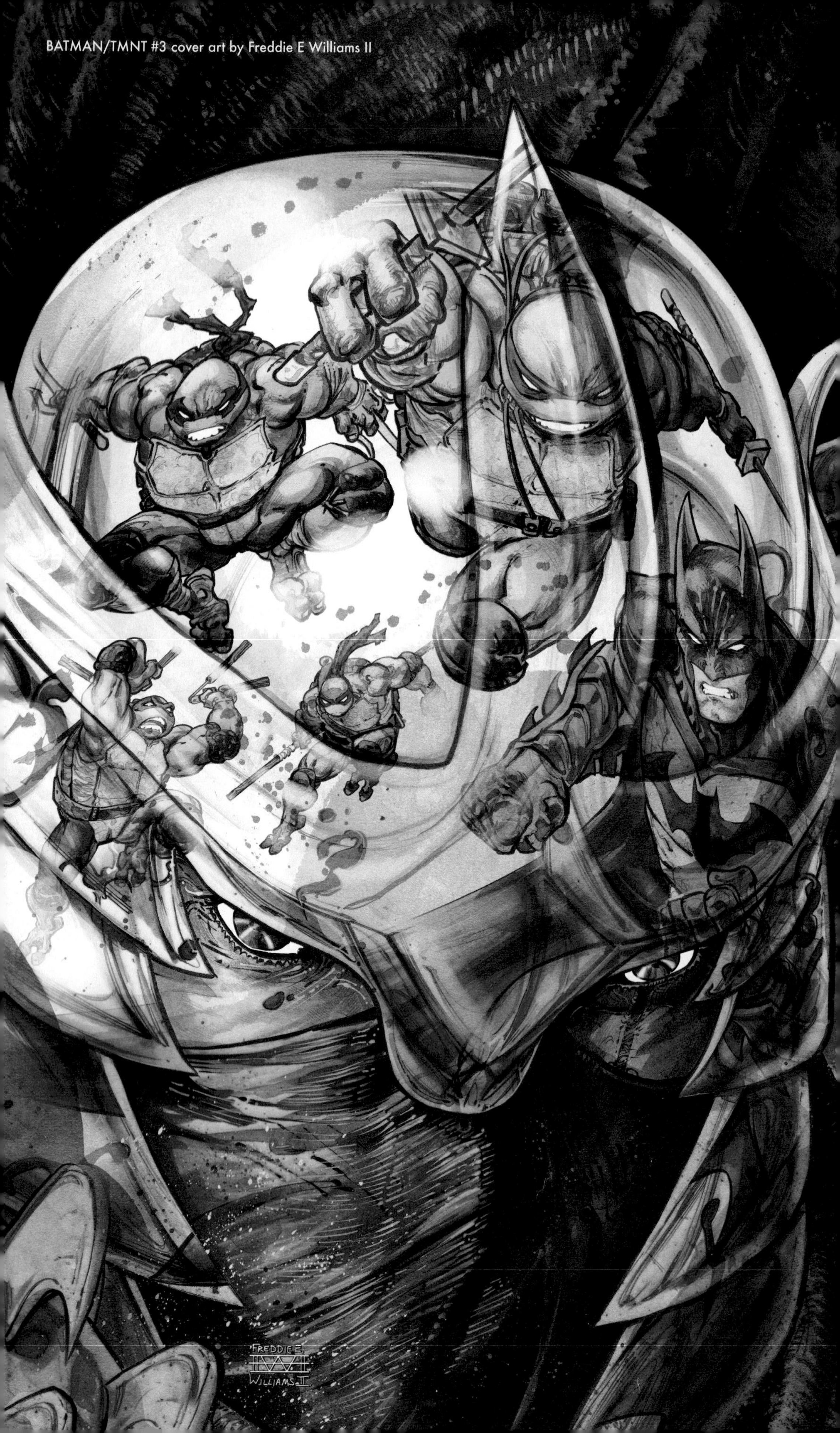

BATMAN/TMNT #3 cover art by Freddie E Williams II

ATMAN/TMNT #3 variant cover art by Kevin Eastman and Tomi Varga

BATMAN/TMNT #3 variant cover art by David Finch

BATMAN/TMNT #3 2nd printing cover art by Freddie E Williams II

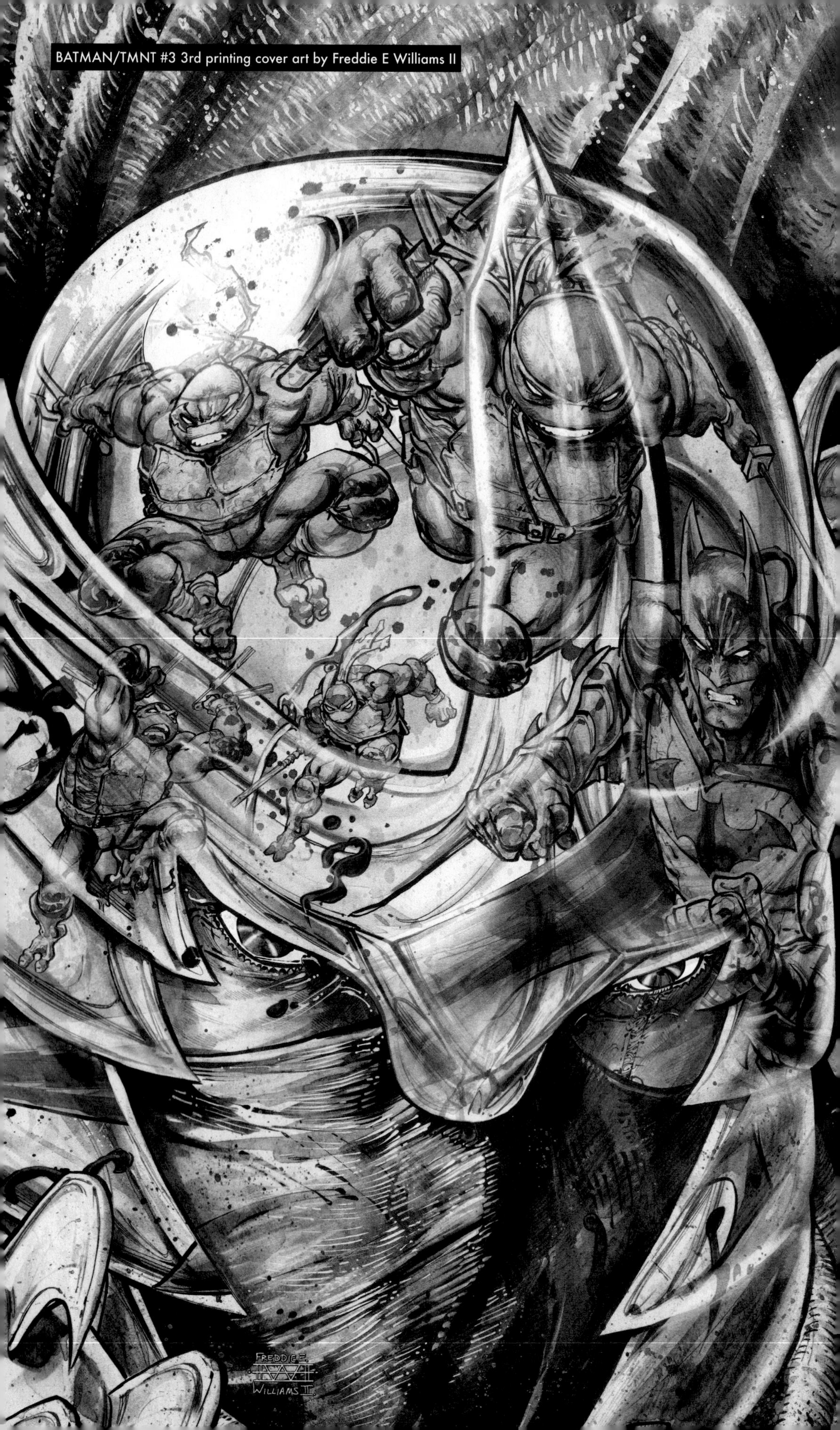

BATMAN/TMNT #3 3rd printing cover art by Freddie E Williams II

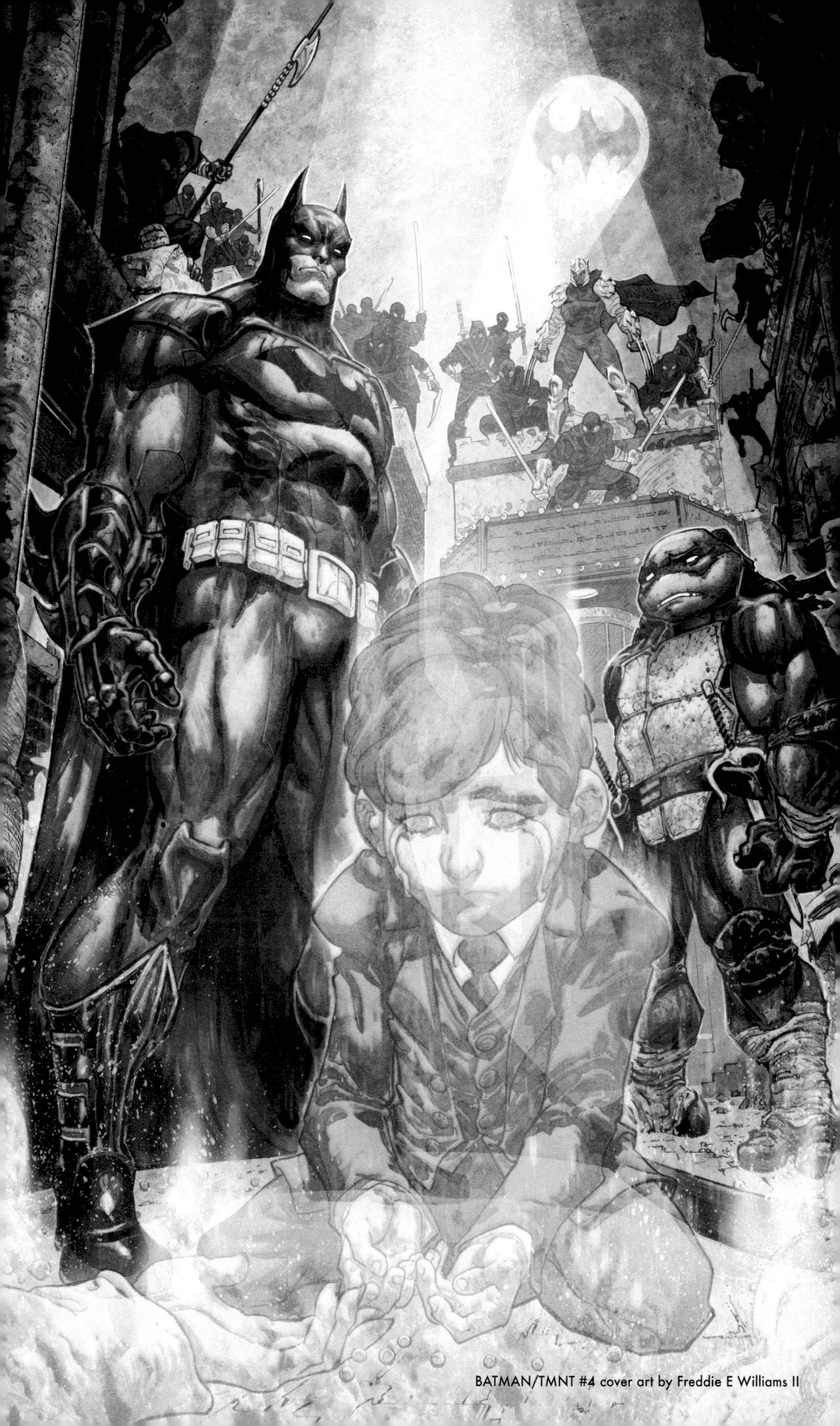

BATMAN/TMNT #4 cover art by Freddie E Williams II

BATMAN/TMNT #4 variant cover art by Kevin Eastman and Tomi Varga

BATMAN/TMNT #4 2nd printing cover art by Freddie E Williams II

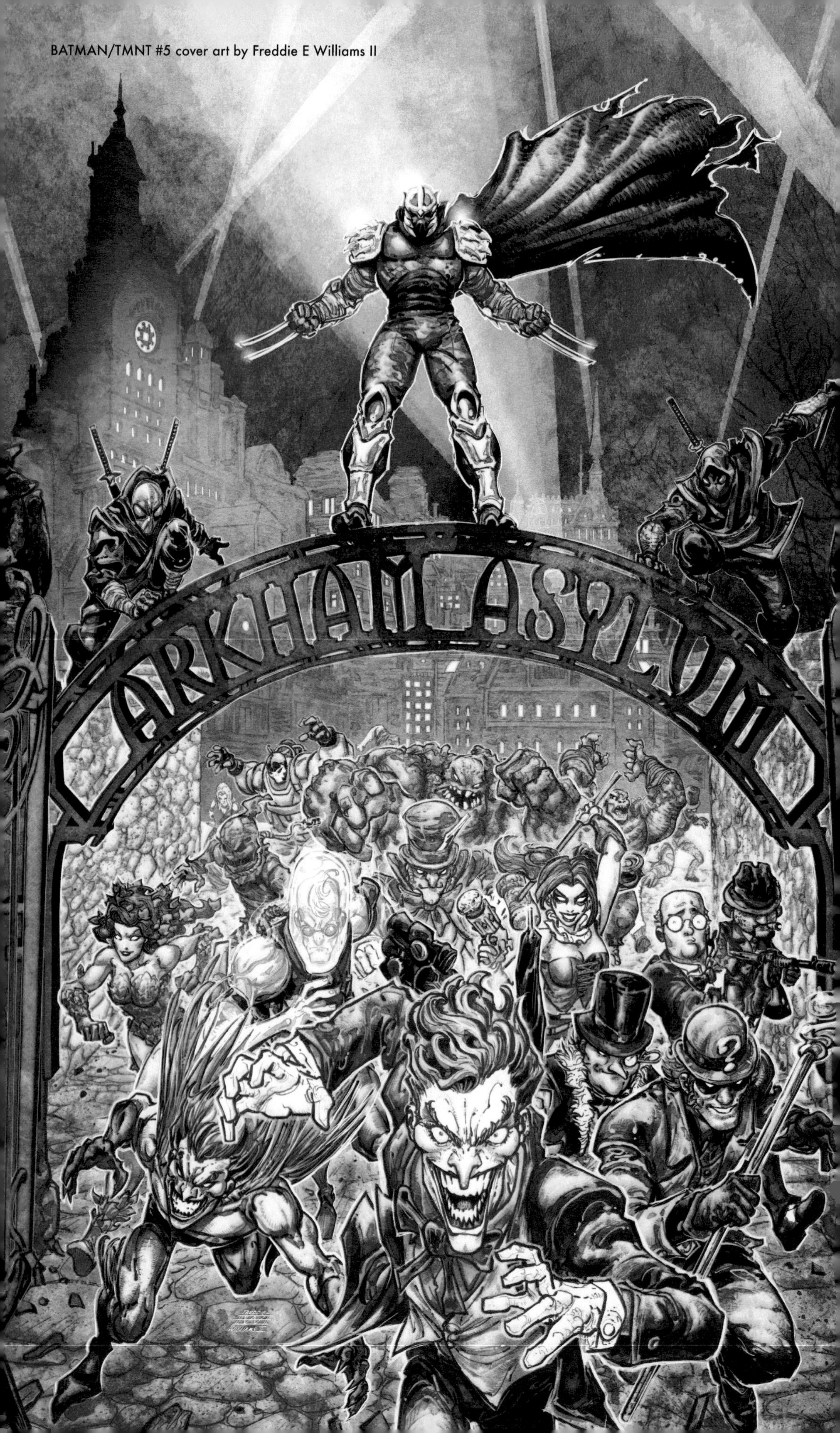

BATMAN/TMNT #5 cover art by Freddie E Williams II

BATMAN/TMNT #5 variant cover art by Kevin Eastman and Tomi Varga

BATMAN/TMNT #6 cover art by Freddie E Williams II

BATMAN/TMNT #6 variant cover art by
Kevin Eastman and Tomi Varga

WWW.FREDDIEART.COM
BATMAN/TMNT
DONATELLO STUDY
FREDDIE E. WILLIAMS II
IDW
FREDDIE E. WILLIAMS II
WWW.FREDDIEART.COM
Donatello © Viacom
WWW.FREDDIEART.COM
BATMAN/TMNT
LEONARDO STUDY
FREDDIE E. WILLIAMS
FREDDIE E. WILLIAMS II
WWW.FREDDIEART.COM
Leonardo © Viacom
WWW.FREDDIEART.COM
BATMAN/TMNT
MICHAELANGELO STUDY
FREDDIE E. WILLIAMS II
IDW
FREDDIE E. WILLIAMS II
WWW.FREDDIEART.COM
Michelangelo © Viacom
WWW.FREDDIEART.COM
BATMAN/TMNT
RAPHAEL STUDY
FREDDIE E. WILLIAMS II
WWW.FREDDIEART.COM
Raphael © Viacom

WWW.FREDDIEART.COM
BATMAN / TMNT
BOOK
BATMAN
ISSUE #
STUDY
PAGE #
FREDDIE E. WILLIAMS II
ARTIST(S)
IDW
PUBLISHING
FOR COVER APPROXIMATE LOGO AREA
FOR FULL BLEED ART DRAW TO SOLID BLEED LINE
FREDDIE E. WILLIAMS II
CUT AND ABUT
TAPE ON BACK
WWW.FREDDIEART.COM
Batman © DC Comics

WWW.FREDDIEART.COM
BATMAN/TMNT
CASEY JONES STUDY
FREDDIE E. WILLIAMS II
FREDDIE E. WILLIAMS II
WWW.FREDDIEART.COM
Casey Jones © Viacom
WWW.FREDDIEART.COM
BATMAN/TMNT
ROBIN
STUDY
FREDDIE E. WILLIAMS II
WWW.FREDDIEART.COM
Robin © DC Comics
WWW.FREDDIEART.COM
BATMAN/TMNT
SHREDDER STUDY
FREDDIE E. WILLIAMS II
FREDDIE E. WILLIAMS II
WWW.FREDDIEART.COM
Shredder © Viacom
WWW.FREDDIEART.COM
BATMAN/TMNT
SPLINTER STUDY
WWW.FREDDIEART.COM
Splinter © Viacom

FREDDIE E. WILLIAMS II

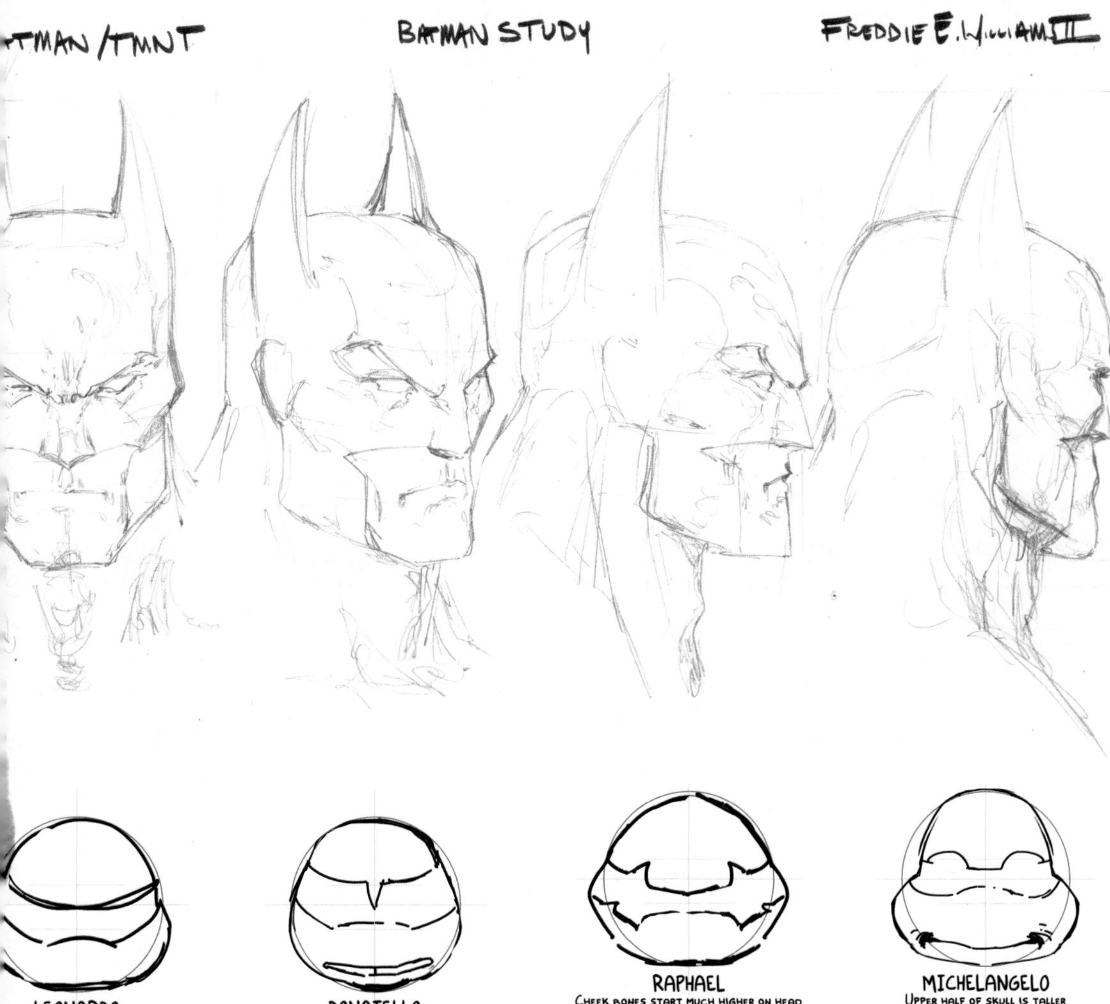
/TMNT
BATMAN STUDY
FREDDIE E. WILLIAMS II
LEONARDO
BANDANA = STRAIGHT SHOOTER
EASTMAN / LAIRD FACE SHAPE
DONATELLO
TALL HEAD, MORE PEAR SHAPED
DIP IN BANDANA POINTING
AT GAP IN TEETH
RAPHAEL
CHEEK BONES START MUCH HIGHER ON HEAD
SLIGHT ANGULAR POINTS AT TOP AND SIDES OF HEAD
BANDANA HAS PEAKS LIKE A DOMINO / WOLVERINE MASK
THE MOST TATTERED BANDANA OF THE TURTLES
MICHELANGELO
UPPER HALF OF SKULL IS TALLER
BIG CHEEKS FOR SMILING
ROUNDED EYEBROWS ON MASK, FOR A HAPPIER LOOK

SHREDDER WINS!
FREDDIE E. WILLIAMS II
FREDDIE E. WILLIAMS II 2014